The Met
ropolitan
Opera

Crosswords for Opera Lovers

DAVID J. KAHN

STERLING
New York

STERLING
New York

An Imprint of Sterling Publishing
387 Park Avenue South
New York, NY 10016

Cover and interior design by Jen Cogliantry Design

Front cover photograph: A scene from Wagner's Das Rheingold
© Ken Howard/Metropolitan Opera
Back cover photograph: The Metropolitan Opera House at night
© Jonathan Tichler/Metropolitan Opera

ISBN 978-1-4027-8757-7

Distributed in Canada by Sterling Publishing
℅ Canadian Manda Group, 165 Dufferin Street
Toronto, Ontario, Canada M6K 3H6
Distributed in the United Kingdom by GMC Distribution Services
Castle Place, 166 High Street, Lewes, East Sussex, England BN7 1XU
Distributed in Australia by Capricorn Link (Australia) Pty. Ltd.
P.O. Box 704, Windsor, NSW 2756, Australia

For information about custom editions, special sales, and premium and
corporate purchases, please contact Sterling Special Sales at 800-805-5489
or specialsales@sterlingpublishing.com.

Printed in Canada

2 4 6 8 10 9 7 5 3 1

www.sterlingpublishing.com

Contents

Introduction

5

Puzzles

6

Answers

86

INTRODUCTION

I t's hard to say who's more devoted: opera lovers or crossword enthusiasts. Opera offers a unique combination of music and drama that can quickly turn into a lifetime passion. And crossword puzzles generate obsessions of their own, creating pencil-wielding addicts by the millions. Now these two pastimes are coming together in the first authoritative crossword book for opera fans.

The puzzles in this book have been created to engage your knowledge of opera, with a special focus on the 2011–12 season of the Metropolitan Opera, the world's largest opera company. Whether you're a longtime opera-goer or a newcomer, you'll find plenty to challenge, reward, and entertain you. Test your puzzle-solving skills with clues about famous artists, historic firsts, opera in the movies, and more.

There are 40 puzzles in this book that increase in difficulty as you go along. So get started now solving these operatic challenges. *In bocca al lupo!*

Moonstruck

The world's most popular opera continues to charm, seduce, and even surprise audiences.

Across

1 Class assignment
7 Musical units
11 Burgundy buddy
14 Conductor Toscanini
15 Kind of blanket
17 Residence in 18-Across
18 Most frequently produced opera in the Met's history
19 Soprano Beverly
21 Caravan stop
22 Former lover of 54-Across
26 Likely
27 Place for a bracelet
28 Opera house feature
31 "Now I get it!"
34 Physicist Bohr
35 Raised to the third power, in math
36 Chest muscle, for short
37 "How sweet ____!"
38 Setting of 18-Across
39 Tiff
40 A Bobbsey twin
41 Sphere or cone
42 Get going
43 Foolish one
44 Foolish
45 Permit
46 Old spy org.
47 Poet who loves 12-Down
49 Pessimist's words

52 Galileo was one
54 Roommate of 47-Across
56 Like the 17-Across
61 Words from a door opener?
62 Book before Jeremiah
63 Ballot marks
64 Constructions at the Met
65 Spectral types

Down

1 Fall behind
2 Chapter in history
3 Orch. section
4 California's Big ____
5 Electra's brother
6 Untagged, in a game
7 "The ____ Song" (*Lakmé* aria)
8 "Sad to say ..."
9 Yank's foe
10 Dished out, as ice cream
11 Greek war god
12 18-Across heroine
13 Decorates a cake
16 Not this
20 Famed Milan opera house
22 "Che gelida ____" (18-Across aria)
23 Hall-of-Fame QB Johnny
24 Balls of yarn
25 Building additions

Answer on page 86

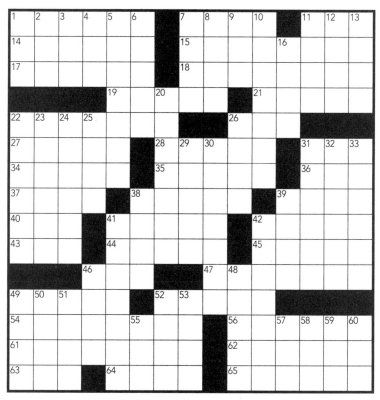

26 Gets older
29 Where 18-Across premiered (1896)
30 Patient ones
31 Horrify
32 Learn about indirectly
33 When the 50-Down scene takes place
38 Coloratura Lily ____
39 Normandy invasion town
41 The fiancées in *Così fan tutte*, e.g.
42 Blue state?

46 Formerly
48 Stick one's ____ (interfere)
49 Giant-screen theater
50 Scene in 18-Across
51 Opera and the like
52 Opera libretto inclusion
53 Debtor's notes
55 Drano component
57 Rebellious Turner
58 Spanish aunt
59 Musical gift
60 Some A.L. batters

Start-Ups

This puzzle celebrates exciting, sometimes nerve-wracking, always notable debut performances at the Met.

Across

1 Bottle tops
5 *Ring* cycle stories, e.g.
10 Life stories
14 Hawaiian port city
15 WWII German sub
16 Jane Austen novel
17 Latin lover's word?
18 Baritone who made his Met debut in *The Ghosts of Versailles* (1995)
20 Musical inspired by *La Bohème*
21 General on a Chinese menu
22 Spring in the Sahara?
23 Soprano who made her Met debut in *Un Ballo in Maschera* (1991)
27 Delivery vehicle
28 Phone no. add-ons
29 French king
32 Dinner fowl
35 Musical threesome
36 Aid
37 With 39-Across, tenor who made his Met debut in *Adriana Lecouvreur* (1968)
39 See 37-Across
41 Mont Blanc, to locals
42 *Picnic* playwright
44 I, historically

45 Manuscript encl.
46 Very energetic
47 Turf
48 Soprano who made her Met debut in *War and Peace* (2002)
53 Puccini opera
56 English cathedral city
57 _____ *Lisa*
58 Bass-baritone who made his Met debut in *Le Nozze di Figaro* (1994)
61 *Prince* _____ (Borodin opera)
62 Rational
63 Pat or Daniel
64 Scrabble piece
65 Argued, as a case
66 _____ *Godunov* (Mussorgsky opera)
67 Gripped

Down

1 Swiss _____ (vegetable)
2 Singer Mann
3 Alternative strategy
4 Quietly, in music
5 Beachgoer's goal
6 Embarrass
7 Recovered from
8 Response to a back rub
9 Depot: Abbr.

Answer on page 88

10 Fathered, in the Bible
11 Radio jock Don
12 Prefix with potent
13 Without: French
19 Christmas drinks
24 Eastern princess: Var.
25 Water or rust
26 "Was ____ loud?"
29 With 34-Down, bass who made his Met debut in *Die Zauberflöte* (1995)
30 *Eugene Onegin* contralto
31 Device with earbuds
32 Some auditors, briefly
33 Milan's Teatro ____ Scala
34 See 29-Down
35 Island east of Fiji

36 German composer Paul ____
38 Singer Celine
40 Othello was one
43 Been attracted to
46 Pesky flier
47 Shag and beehive, say
48 Pimply
49 Nicholas Gage memoir
50 Hollywood nickname of the '50s
51 Small hill
52 Rowed
53 Recipe amt.
54 Spoken
55 "Auld Lang ____"
59 Recede
60 Aussie hopper

9

Promises, Promises

A vulnerable young girl and a callous visitor are a tragic combination.

Across

1 Expensive fur
6 Stereo part
9 17-Across's country
14 Vocally
15 "Tu che a ____" (*Lucia di Lammermoor* aria)
16 Friend in a sombrero
17 Heroine of a 40-Across opera
19 Windmill features
20 Drew even again
21 Not spare the rod
23 New Age superstar
24 Met website address ending
27 Chilean range
29 Employee's complaint, maybe
32 Saudi, e.g.
34 It's a no-no
37 Western wine valley
38 1944 battle site
39 Buckeyes' sch.
40 See 26-Down
43 Lubricate
44 Source of *Das Rheingold*
46 Like show horses
47 Part of a pound
49 ____ noire (bugaboo)
50 Four-bagger
52 Concise

54 Lode deposit
55 Cutting remark
59 Look that's in again
61 Tiny organisms
63 Muscular
65 U.S. consul in 36-Down
68 Tuckered out
69 Natural tanner
70 "It's ____!"
71 Mezzo-soprano DiDonato
72 Accessory for 17-Across
73 Draw a bead on

Down

1 "____ bleu!"
2 1979 sci-fi chiller
3 Pirate's prize
4 Tenor Pavarotti
5 Emmy winner Falco
6 TV spots
7 Soccer star Hamm
8 French-born Met diva
9 Certain Indonesian
10 Actresses Plummer and Peet
11 Whom 17-Across loved
12 Get better, as wine
13 Negatives
18 Smell
22 Song of praise
25 Gaucho's workplace

Answer on page 90

26 With 40-Across, composer of 36-Down
28 _____ law (old Germanic legal code)
30 Alley _____
31 Web designer?
33 Tree trunk
34 Last scene in *Lucia di Lammermoor*
35 So far
36 *Madama* _____ (nickname of 17-Across, and theme of this puzzle)
41 Opera house employee
42 Letters on a chit

45 Nonconformist
48 Famous aria sung by 17-Across
51 Bring up
53 Broadway composer Jule
56 Crosswise to a ship
57 Bob Marley fan
58 Harass
60 _____ buco (veal dish)
62 Movie rating org.
63 *The* _____ (Uris novel)
64 "Xanadu" band, for short
66 Busy airport
67 *Wheel of Fortune* request

Surname Game

'S wonderful, 's marvelous, 'Schicchi! These operatic heroes' last names might have more than one meaning.

Across

1 Cohort of Clark
5 Rent-____
9 Heavy haulers
14 Upscale hotel name
15 *Lohengrin* soprano
16 Hackneyed
17 *Candide* composer
19 Let in
20 Second delay of a Tchaikovsky opera?
22 Clinton years, e.g.
23 Poem of praise
24 Number of 33-Acrosses in Verdi's *Macbeth*
27 Author John Dickson ____
29 Baths
33 Opera segment
34 Slightly
36 Think creatively
38 Music critic's review of a Britten opera?
41 Market trader
42 A whole bunch
43 U.S.N.A. grad
44 Nabisco cookie
45 Have to have
47 Views
48 Soak (up)
49 Muscle-builder's pride

51 Music critic's review of a Mussorgsky opera?
59 Opium flower
60 Opera composer Luigi
61 Betray, in a way
62 Suspend
63 Pub quaffs
64 Cybermemo
65 Stick around
66 Antitoxins

Down

1 Gray wolf
2 Portent
3 About, in a memo
4 Opera cast member
5 Big name in insurance
6 Antony's love, for short
7 "You wish!"
8 Sought, as office
9 With 13-Down, opera props and scenery
10 *Ring* cycle goddess
11 She dies at the end of *La Bohème*
12 "Put ____ writing"
13 See 9-Down
18 Title for Rudolf Bing
21 Unanchored
24 String bean's opposite
25 Autumn shade
26 Helpful

Answer on page 92

27 Real heel
28 Confuse
29 Sun. delivery
30 Check recipient
31 Do penance
32 Dr. for kids
34 Pres. Lincoln
35 Activate
37 Galas
39 ____-mo
40 Lawn makeup
46 Important periods
47 Diving devices

48 *Funny Girl* composer
49 Gershwin opera hero
50 Univ. e-mail address part
51 Soprano Sutherland
52 ____ no good
53 Smudge
54 "Take ____!"
55 Actress Rowlands
56 River in *Aida*
57 Humdinger
58 Amex alternative
59 Historical start?

Over the Top

This shocking melodrama has been titillating, offending, and enthralling audiences since its premiere in Rome in 1900.

Across

1 Desertlike
5 Occupation of 17-Across
11 Gunpowder unit
14 ____-majesté
15 Put into a crate
16 ____ du Diable
17 Heroine of a Puccini opera set in Rome in 1800
19 Indian bread
20 Feel sick
21 Phobos orbits it
22 Not weighing much
24 See 29-Down
26 Interminably
28 Suffix with election
29 Bits of wit
32 ____ States (central Italy in 1800)
35 Suffragist Carrie
36 Melville novel
37 Not much
38 With 56-Across, lover of 17-Across
39 Soprano from New Jersey
40 Roman historian
41 Atop
42 Marching band members
43 Tries to get a better view from, maybe
45 Sign of a hit at the Met
46 Where Joan of Arc died

47 Occupation of 38-/56-Across
51 Tonio, in *Pagliacci*
53 Valley
54 "That feels so good"
55 On fire
56 See 38-Across
60 Defib operator
61 Trued up: Var.
62 Hammer part
63 Cio-Cio-San's sash
64 See 11-Down
65 ____ Stanley Gardner

Down

1 Code words for "A"
2 Vestige
3 Sicily, to Sicilians
4 ____ Rosenkavalier (Richard Strauss opera)
5 Coastal atmosphere
6 Prefix with coastal
7 Sgts. and the like
8 Good time, slangily
9 Upper-left key
10 Old Spanish coins
11 With 64-Across, occupier of Rome in 1798
12 Valley where David slew Goliath
13 Fellow
18 Motivate

Answer on page 94

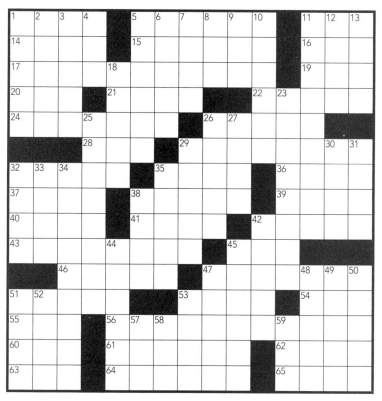

23 Not still
25 "All set to go?"
26 Away
27 Not tricked by
29 With 24-Across, adversary
    of 38-/56-Across
30 Vocal quality
31 High-protein beans
32 Buddies
33 Fighting
34 Tenor whose last role
    at the Met was 56-Across
35 Bird on a menu
38 Ponder

42 Like onion rings
44 Victim of Macbeth
45 Lunches for dieters
47 French city, in song
48 Police stunner
49 Prop for a 47-Across
50 River that inspired a
    Ring opera
51 Queenly role for Liz
52 Arm or leg
53 Boone, to rustics
57 In the style of
58 Big shot, for short
59 Unclose, poetically

Picture This

Opera and the movies have had a love affair from the days of the silents to today's *Live in HD* transmissions into movie theaters.

Across

1 Kind of metabolism
6 "I dare you!"
10 Grouchy one
14 Sprang up
15 *Das Rheingold* deity
16 Conceal
17 Roberto Benigni movie, with music from *Les Contes d'Hoffmann*
20 Computer input
21 Big name in chips
22 Neither partner
24 Outback runner
25 Michael Douglas movie, with music from *Rigoletto*
31 Cop's collar
35 Mirror _____
36 Yemen's capital city
38 Stephen of *The Crying Game*
39 Glenn Close movie, with music from *Madama Butterfly*
43 Before, in verse
44 Turkish currency
45 Certain belly button
46 Play area
48 Robert De Niro movie, with music from *Cavalleria Rusticana*
51 Sunbeam

53 Reverse of WSW
54 Witty Wilde
57 Deli hangers
63 Bruce Willis movie, with music from *Lucia di Lammermoor*
67 Lease
68 Russian prince of opera
69 Valuable violin
70 _____ and sciences
71 Salon job
72 Met supporter, say

Down

1 The _____ Soprano (Ionesco play)
2 Met highlight
3 With 29-Down, low-pressure pitch
4 On the ocean
5 Luau gifts
6 One who's short?
7 Bauxite, e.g.
8 Boise's locale: Abbr.
9 Letter after sigma
10 "Don't be discouraged"
11 Break in relations
12 Together, to Toscanini
13 *Lakmé*'s "_____ Song"
18 E-mail folder
19 Tiny _____ Cratchit

Answer on page 86

23 Do an opera director's job, maybe
24 Sicilian spouter
25 Judy Blume bestseller
26 Soprano Lucine, a longtime Met favorite
27 "Ciao!"
28 N.Y.C. airport
29 See 3-Down
30 Canal site
32 Verdi aria
33 Apply more grease
34 Group of experts
37 Slip _____ (err)
40 Like light opera songs
41 _____-la-la

42 Bath
47 Early versions
49 Advertising section
50 Oscar winner Patricia
52 *Exodus* hero
54 Other, in Oaxaca
55 Theater/opera director Bartlett _____
56 Penny
58 Diva's role, usually
59 Bullets and the like
60 Like opera villains
61 Fascinated by
62 Hoo-ha
64 In shape
65 _____ Friday's
66 Snookums

The Fallen Woman

Sometimes the noblest gestures come from the most unexpected people.

Across

1 Waikiki welcome
4 Commotion
8 Feels sorry for
14 Golfer Ernie
15 Dublin's home
16 Bogged down
17 With 19-Across, heroine of 50-Across
19 See 17-Across
20 Cove
21 Nary a soul
23 Drops off
24 17-/19-Across and others
29 "____ tú" (1974 hit song)
30 Choir voices
31 Born
32 Fairy tale villains
34 Operatic hero, often
36 With 39-Across, nobleman who loves 17-/19-Across
39 See 36-Across
41 Gertrude, in *Roméo et Juliette*
42 Duplicate copy
43 Italian ____
44 Gas bill unit
46 Spanish snack
50 Verdi opera, and this puzzle's title, in Italian
53 Reply to "That so?"
54 Tricky turns

55 Aria parts
56 City where 50-Across premiered (1853)
59 Teatro ____ (opera house where 50-Across premiered)
62 Playground retort
63 Basso Pinza
64 Allow
65 Events in some romantic operas
66 Blubbers
67 Pompous fool

Down

1 Maestro James
2 *Sense and Sensibility* protagonist
3 Princess in a Wagner opera
4 Pedal pushers
5 Turned on
6 Display at N.Y.C.'s other Met
7 Woodstock's home?
8 Basketball moves
9 Cockamamie
10 Grimm collections
11 Wrath
12 Switz. locale
13 Hog haven
18 Landlords

Answer on page 88

22 _____ *y plata* (Montana's motto)
24 Ace or ten
25 Margarine
26 _____ Domini
27 Gas light
28 Spanish muralist
33 German capital?
34 Number before *quattro*
35 Diva's forte
36 Shade of blue
37 Brasi of *The Godfather*
38 Stew
39 Encircled
40 Thompson who played 2-Down on screen

42 It's spotted on kids
44 Soap boxes?
45 Hurry
47 Title role in a Verdi opera
48 *Five Easy* _____
49 Stocks and such
51 Jockey straps
52 Fancy tie
55 Revivalists
56 Wine holder
57 Blunder
58 Napoleonic marshal
60 _____ dye (chemical coloring)
61 Little lie

Letters from the Big Apple

The Met—it's Gotham's greatest opera company.

Across

1 Each
5 Angular start?
8 New York's _____ Zee Bridge
14 Role in Prokofiev's *War and Peace*
16 Opera based on a Shakespeare play
17 Imaginary
18 Opera's Tebaldi
19 Actress MacGraw
20 Hereditary
22 Molecular matter
23 Introvert
25 Lyricist Gershwin
27 Like New York City (and whose letters comprise every answer in this puzzle)
35 Give marks to
38 Improviser's asset
39 _____ acid
40 Having wings
41 Subject of many a 49-Across
44 _____ time (never)
45 Tag words?
47 Small gripe
48 Gripe
49 Art form since the 17th century

53 Swiss peak
54 End of _____
58 High C, e.g.
62 Like some patches
66 Matchsticks game
67 Title role in a 2001 French comedy
69 Helena resident
71 Contralto Anderson
72 Peasant in *L'Elisir d'Amore*
73 Opera whose protagonist dies in his lover's arms
74 Land in *la mer*
75 Feminist Lucretia

Down

1 One-year record
2 Goldsmith in *Simon Boccanegra*
3 Choose to participate
4 Luau dish
5 Where Dollywood is: Abbr.
6 Horse color
7 *To Live and Die* _____
8 Caped fighter
9 With 36-Down, pigged out
10 Clinton cabinet member Federico
11 Piece of real estate
12 Voice below soprano
13 Linguist Chomsky
15 French wine valley

Answer on page 90

21 It may be 20%
24 Chef Lagasse
26 Chicken-king connection
28 Earl Grey, say
29 Hit head-on
30 Maine college town
31 1965 Yardbirds hit
32 *La Clemenza di* _____ (Mozart opera)
33 Soprano Moffo
34 Midday
35 Hindu royal
36 See 9-Down
37 "Toodles"
42 Tear
43 Summer in Paris
46 Actress Carrere

50 _____ juris (under another's control)
51 Broadcaster of Met happenings
52 Totaled, costwise
55 Movie composer Morricone
56 Laughing
57 "I _____ kidding!"
58 Tattle on
59 Actor Sharif
60 Shore bird
61 Director Kazan
63 Old Dodge model
64 Carol
65 "This one's _____"
68 Suffix with Freud
70 Outfielder's asset

Out of Africa

This heroine made her debut in Cairo in 1871.

Across

1 Indulge
8 Bug
15 Aria's effect, often
16 Usually
17 Egyptian who loves 57-Down
18 What 57-Down means, in Arabic
19 Times remembered
20 Chemical endings
22 A lot
23 Put into words
24 _____ Spumante
26 Power glitch
27 Bathroom fixture
30 Site of the Real Teatro di San Carlo opera house
33 Opera by 59-Down
38 Neutral shade
39 Composer of 57-Down
41 Billfold bills
42 Oscar-winning role for Colin Firth
44 Divas sometimes make them
46 One way to get up
48 Help desk sign
52 British prep since 1440
53 Hush-hush job
56 Move, to a Realtor
57 Swiss river

59 Peel
60 Setting of 57-Down
62 Egyptian princess who loves 17-Across
65 Groups of nine
66 Regatta, e.g.
67 Step on it
68 Turbojets and the like

Down

1 First known asteroid
2 Soprano who was a memorable 57-Down
3 NBC morning show
4 Greek vowels
5 Canyon feature
6 Boot part
7 Like some inspections
8 Informal greeting
9 Goddess worshiped in 57-Down
10 College dorm figures: Abbr.
11 *Un Ballo in Maschera* aria
12 Coach
13 Go _____ (agree)
14 By itself
21 View from 60-Across
24 MSN rival
25 Turn
26 _____ Lanka
27 Backstage treat at the Met

Answer on page 92

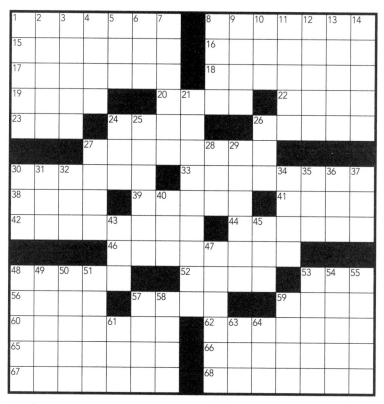

28 Flower starter
29 Blue blood, informally
30 Less than zero: Abbr.
31 Expert
32 Expert
34 One taking action
35 Travel guide listing
36 Chorus opening?
37 Chorus closing?
40 Raiser of Cain
43 "Golly!"
45 With 63-Down, swindlers
47 Relaxed
48 Ready for battle

49 "I ____ reason why ..."
50 Alphabet string
51 Sulking type
53 Kitchen wrap brand
54 Soprano who was a memorable 57-Down
55 *Sí* and *oui*
57 This puzzle's theme
58 Aide: Abbr.
59 Pioneer opera composer Jacopo ____
61 Prosciutto, e.g.
63 See 45-Down
64 Old horse

Firsts

In its 128-year history, the Met has seen countless career-changing moments.

Across

1 Afrikaner
5 "____ babbino caro" (Puccini aria)
9 ____ Caldwell, first female conductor at the Met (1976)
14 With 70-Across, first Met opera at Lincoln Center (1966)
16 Cheery song syllables
17 First opera broadcast from the Met on radio (1931)
19 Symbol of slowness
20 Hook's henchman
21 Give the boot
22 N.Y. Met, e.g.
25 Take ____ (snooze)
27 Lettuce variety
30 Luggage attachment
34 Resident of 35-Across
35 First place?
37 Brain protector
38 Zeffirelli's 1982 *La Traviata*, e.g.
40 Caught some Z's
43 Bluesy James
44 Not yet up
46 Telegram
48 French possessive
49 Joining (up)

52 Movie promos
54 Locket shape
55 "Take this!"
56 Be shy, maybe
59 It's an OK city
61 Massenet opera
65 Conductor who made his first Met appearance in 1908
69 First-ever opera at the Met (1883)
70 See 14-Across
71 Cloak-and-dagger types
72 President
73 Cio-Cio-San, for one

Down

1 Scrooge outbursts
2 ____ even keel
3 European smoker?
4 Count Almaviva's bride, in a Rossini opera
5 Olive ____
6 When repeated, a card game
7 Alehouses
8 One who's "out"
9 Waterways
10 "You ____ here"
11 Pro follower
12 *Roots* author Haley
13 Hearty partner

Answer on page 94

15 With 29-Down, the Met's original Mimi in *La Bohème*
18 _____ Lee Nolin of *Baywatch*
23 Extremities
24 Barn dance
26 Small breed, informally
27 Change equipment
28 Sheeplike
29 See 15-Down
31 Last word of a Mozart opera title
32 Change
33 *The Voyage* composer Philip
36 Straight out of the box
39 Staff note
41 Central part

42 Alder or elder
45 Redirects
47 Cold-weather cap feature
50 iPod type
51 Bug
53 Spotted in the area of
56 Klutzy sorts
57 Trendy sandwich
58 Sewing case
60 1996 presidential also-ran
62 Refer to
63 Concerning
64 Gorilla watcher Fossey
66 Play for a fool
67 Bounding main
68 Atlantic catch

Cutting Edge

Everyone wants him, everyone calls him: this man is at the center of opera's most enduringly successful comedy.

Across

1 Bay windows
7 ____ *Troyens* (Berlioz opera)
10 Monopoly token
14 Airport pickup
15 Clark's *Mogambo* co-star
16 Singer Perry
17 Protagonist of 40-Across
18 Cashed in
20 Musician Brian
21 Leoncavallo opera, familiarly
23 Bank rights
24 Hot blue spectral type
27 Composer of 40-Across
30 *Manon* ____ (Puccini opera)
32 Quirk
35 Salad green
38 Wrangler rival
39 Appraise
40 English title of a comic opera that premiered in 1816, with *The*
43 Prefix with dextrous
44 G.P. gp.
45 Old record components
46 Vote for
47 Bundles
49 Peters who was a notable 64-Across at the Met

52 Blue Cross alternative
56 Divided
58 Pay extender?
60 Cleanse (of)
61 Handy item for a handyman
64 Ward of 37-Down
67 *Vogue* competitor
68 "That means ____!"
69 For the time being, for short
70 ____ court
71 Popular street name
72 Passover dinners

Down

1 *L'*____ (Monteverdi opera)
2 Harness parts
3 Gold bar
4 Fraternity letter
5 Choreographer Lubovitch
6 Pigpen food
7 Aria sung by 17-Across
8 Christmas ____
9 Like many operas
10 Leave stranded during cold weather, say
11 Where 40-Across premiered
12 Sign of things to come
13 Go-ahead cues
19 Certain Ivy Leaguer

Answer on page 86

22 Part of a circle
25 Cover story?
26 Debussy's "dream"
28 Petitions
29 Stow in a ship's hold
31 Colorful shawl
33 "_____ never work!"
34 So-so grades
35 "Buy It Now" site
36 Big star
37 Rival of Count Almaviva, in 40-Across
39 Dentist's request
41 General Bradley

42 Life, to 27-Across
48 _____ Kan dog food
50 Baby screecher
51 Hope or Barker
53 Unoriginal
54 West Coast gridder
55 *Nixon in China* composer
56 News clipping
57 Court plea, informally
59 Some Dada works
62 Cone site
63 Online chuckle
65 Mined-over matter?
66 Yard material

Noteworthy People

When you know the notes to sing—you can name most anybody in this puzzle.

Across

1 BBC import, briefly
5 One of the Baldwins
9 Mojave home
14 Spa wear
15 Ritzy
16 *Two Women* Oscar winner
17 Melody for Melba
18 Tenor whose name is Spanish for "calm Sunday"
20 Soprano Rysanek
22 Cincinnati-to-New York dir.
23 Coward of the theater
24 Buildups on jackets
26 Everest climbs, e.g.
28 Some tunas
31 ____ kwon do
32 Things with strings
33 Canine from Kansas
35 Setting of *Idomeneo*
39 Common batteries
40 Conductor who won 31 Grammys
42 Way out
43 *The Bartered* ____ (Smetana opera)
45 Painter of dreamscapes
46 Ring contest
47 Neighbor of Que.
49 Human-powered taxis
51 Like Don Giovanni

55 Relish
56 Fancy marbles
57 Opera's Pinkerton, and others: Abbr.
59 Noggin
62 1990 Richard Tucker Award winner
65 Tartan design
66 Under, in Italian
67 Mideast carrier
68 In addition
69 Govt. bill
70 Singer Seeger
71 Dappled horse

Down

1 Asia's ____ Sea
2 Yawn producer
3 Principal guest conductor at the Met, starting in 2010
4 Nerdy hats
5 It may be hearty
6 *Damn Yankees* vamp
7 Suffix with opal
8 *Turandot* setting
9 Designer Gucci
10 Be overbearing
11 "Smoking ____?"
12 Sire
13 Organic compounds
19 Act, old-style

Answer on page 88

21 Like Brahms's *Symphony No. 3*
25 Hair net
27 Prickly plants
28 Spill the beans
29 Soprano Evelyn who won a 1966 Grammy
30 Rein, e.g.
34 Eyes
36 Composer of *Fiesque*
37 Temple vault, at the end of *Aida*
38 Love child?
40 UConn women's basketball coach Auriemma
41 Result of some geometric intersections
44 Hall of Fame running back Tony ____
46 Dog walker's item
48 Rock's Jethro ____
50 1961 Nobelist Andric
51 Not moving
52 Massenet opera
53 Have a loan from
54 Pricey
58 Photog's request
60 Brainy Simpson
61 Site of a fall
63 Adversary
64 D.C. swinger?

Let's Make a Deal

The devil appears frequently at the opera, but he is probably most admired for his star turn in this classic French work which opened the Met in 1883.

Across

1 Raga instrument
6 *The Pearl Fishers* composer
11 Performed
14 Lower
15 Type size
16 "Ti ____" (Pavarotti album)
17 Like the evil spirit in 38-Across
20 Patronizes, as a hotel
21 Opera that opens in a Rome church
22 Editor's mark
24 Question starter
25 Heroine of 38-Across
30 Volvo rival
34 Love a lot
35 Component of bronze
36 Sailors' saint
37 With 48-Across, "hello" sticker
38 Gounod work and lead role
40 Bird beaks
41 Type of arch
42 Dipstick coating
43 Noblemen in *Rigoletto*
44 Las Vegas light
45 38-Across, for one
48 See 37-Across
50 Ocho ____, Jamaica

51 Coloratura variations
54 Nibbling (on)
59 Talk like 38-Across?
63 Mozart's home: Abbr.
64 Feld of ballet
65 Speechify
66 Q-U link
67 Auto damage
68 Just know

Down

1 ____ Club (retailer)
2 "Oh, sure!"
3 Toledo tidbit
4 Pale
5 Print again
6 Good way to feel
7 U.N. agcy.
8 Nada
9 Ordinal ending
10 Some canines
11 Speaker's spot
12 Non-PC purchase
13 Spanish Mrs.
18 More than fill
19 Become less tense
23 Like 38-Across's role, e.g.
24 Hit the road
25 1884 opéra comique
26 You can say that again
27 Hero of another Gounod opera

Answer on page 90

28 Popular antioxidant
29 "_____ a pity"
31 How some think
32 Honey-colored
33 _____ nova
38 Verne traveler Phileas
39 Tune
43 Back to back, to Gounod
46 *A Midsummer _____ Dream*
   (Britten opera)
47 Finito

49 Appealed
51 Boris Godunov, for one
52 Numbered work
53 Digs made of twigs
55 Lived
56 _____ *IV* (6-Across opera)
57 Pesky insects
58 Hit TV musical
60 Corrida call
61 End of a French opera?
62 Little squirt

Opening Credits

They'll never forget their first time on the Met stage.

Across

1 Kind of shot
4 October gem
8 *Vanessa* composer
14 Opera house whose name means "the phoenix"
16 Elvira's love in *I Puritani*
17 Ben Heppner's 1991 Met opera debut
18 Seems suspicious
19 100 centavos
20 Nouveau _____
22 Grazing ground
23 Folder labels
26 Angelica, say
28 Sunshine State city, briefly
31 Stephanie Blythe's 1995 Met opera debut
35 Tuna at a sushi bar
36 Ready to pour
38 Old fiddler
39 Renée Fleming's 1991 Met opera debut
43 Yogi Berra had a hand in it
44 _____ eclipse
45 Get bronze
46 Natalie Dessay's 1994 Met opera debut
49 It's taken every ten years
51 Flower holder
52 "Wishing won't make _____"
53 Cargo area
56 Sporting blades
58 Kvetch
62 Supreme Egyptian god: Var.
64 Angela Gheorghiu's 1993 Met opera debut
67 Clapboards, e.g.
68 *Manfred* composer
69 Navy builder
70 Sing like Ella
71 Refrain syllable

Down

1 Somersault
2 Stow on board
3 NASA concern
4 *A Chorus Line* song
5 Wrestler's goal
6 Those who give excellent service?
7 English name of the Pope in *Attila*
8 Critic, and then some
9 Gun suppliers
10 Hwy.
11 Kind of market
12 First name in mystery
13 Soprano Ponselle

Answer on page 92

15 Overact
21 Former Met official Schuyler ____
24 Running the gamut
25 German auto pioneer
27 Met general manager, 1950–72
28 Actress Hayek
29 Not our
30 Columbian ship
31 Where Galileo taught geometry
32 Guinness Book listings
33 Pianist Claudio
34 Crazies
37 "I'm listening"
40 Better places?
41 Almanac bit

42 Angers
47 Forever, in verse
48 Met *Ring* cycle director Robert ____
50 Night, in Nogales
52 Stern with a bow
53 ____-baritone
54 Gallic girlfriend
55 Sci-fi sage
57 Shade providers
59 Money owed to Benoit, in 64-Across
60 Like Nathan Gunn: Abbr.
61 Second of a series
63 Pen point
65 Troop gp.
66 East, in Berlin

The Rake Punished

Opera's greatest lover actually has a terrible time with the ladies in this sly masterpiece.

Across

1 Holed up
4 Where 18-Across premiered (1787)
10 Unaccompanied
14 Lennon's love
15 ____ *Heroes* (1960s sitcom)
16 Badlands feature
17 Pinkerton's org. in *Madama Butterfly*
18 Opera about a libertine who gets his comeuppance
20 Wagner cycle, familiarly
22 ____ *culpa*
23 Good point
24 Riyadh residents
26 They have loads to do
28 Revenging figure of 3-Down's father
29 Lenya of *The Threepenny Opera*
30 Brains
31 Attend
32 Messy dresser
36 Spike TV, once
37 33-Down, to 18-Across
40 Conductor Queler
41 RR stops
43 Roméo, for one
44 Ballyhoos
46 Western pic

48 "Il mio ____ " (18-Across aria)
49 Tasted
52 They settle tabs
53 Really go for
54 Like a 54-Down
55 Move, informally
57 Basso famous for singing 18-Across
61 Livy's law
62 D-Day city
63 Some Starbucks orders
64 Stan of Marvel Comics
65 Roughly
66 Composer of 18-Across
67 Special ____

Down

1 Time piece?
2 Not giving an inch
3 Victim of 18-Across
4 Third degree?
5 One who splits quarters?
6 Mezzo-soprano Baltsa
7 Totally smitten
8 Prefix with sphere
9 With 35-Down, a Paul Anka hit
10 Big successes
11 Wound up
12 *Roots* actor Ed
13 Steps

Answer on page 94

19 Very great
21 Fortitude
25 Club bill
26 20-Across god
27 Loads
28 Retired planes
29 18-Across, notably
31 Avarice
33 18-Across role
34 Ignore an alarm, maybe
35 See 9-Down
38 Novel ending?
39 Place to work out, familiarly
42 3-Down, vocally

45 North Sea feeder
47 Ray or Jay
48 Meddle (with)
49 Vanzetti's partner in anarchy
50 "Be ____ and help me"
51 ____ und Aron (Schoenberg opera)
52 Vatican City draw
54 Airhead
56 Dumb ____ (oafs)
58 Nightmarish street
59 ____ Paulo, Brazil
60 Suffix with capital

Ring Master

This mythological epic is the supreme test for an opera company and one of the grandest theatrical experiences to be had.

Across

1 Hotel amenities
6 Soccer _____
9 Amazed
14 Love, to Luciano
15 "_____ tu" (baritone aria)
16 Explorer Sebastian
17 Rigoletto's daughter
18 Source of stories in the *Ring* cycle
20 Gold standard
22 Like, awesome
23 Express
24 Wing
26 Big fuss
27 Egg: Prefix
28 NBC show since 1975
29 Greet the villain
30 Removing, in a way
31 Toll
33 Adjoining (on)
35 Carnival game
38 Recipe word
39 Farrow and Hamm
41 Marking for life
44 Sound familiar
46 Type of burner
48 Like Saturn
49 Old GM sports car
50 _____ *Rheingold* (*Ring* cycle opera)
53 Onetime telecom giant
54 Capote, on stage
55 Taradiddle
56 Harem room
57 Narc's org.
58 Physician called "the father of modern medicine"
60 Like the *Ring* cycle
63 Big numbers
66 Makeup mishap
67 Golfer's concern
68 Link with
69 Some hook shapes
70 Promgoers: Abbr.
71 Done

Down

1 Slump
2 "Who _____?"
3 Like the *Ring* cycle
4 Goddess in two *Ring* cycle operas
5 Yachting event, e.g.
6 Personally guiding
7 Onetime peso component
8 Imitating
9 Bejeweled, in urban slang
10 1960s war zone
11 Chasm
12 60-Across king of the gods
13 _____ alcohol
19 Enjoying a lot
21 Like many opera fans

Answer on page 86

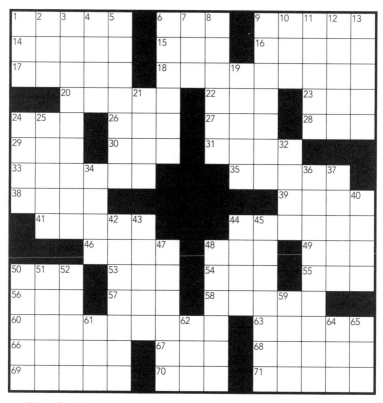

24 Goes back
25 Plunders
32 Act 5 setting in *Roméo et Juliette*
34 Party pooper
36 *Ring* cycle opera
37 1972 missile pact
40 No neatnik
42 1984 Super Bowl champs
43 Illegal bookie, e.g.
44 Experts in deception

45 Look up to
47 Some opposums
48 Cell phone selections
50 Use a divining rod
51 *Doctor Atomic* composer
52 Wise old heads
59 Poetic land
61 Scot's denial
62 Lungful
64 Broke a fast
65 It has roots

Looking Back

The Met has been one of the world's most important opera houses since it opened in 1883.

Across

1 Elk
7 Biol., for one
10 Cooking direction
14 Brought down
15 Soprano who made her 1918 Met debut opposite 64-Across
17 Conductor who once took piano lessons from Rudolf Serkin
18 First African-American to sing at the Met
19 Indian silk center
21 Either of two A.L. teams
22 "Is that ____?"
23 Prokofiev's ____ and Peace
25 Ore suffix
26 Landlord, say
28 Acapulco gold
29 Most high-waisted
32 What every puzzle in this book has
34 Politico Paul
35 Perched on
39 Piedmont city
40 Put up
42 Tail end
43 Wagner's refusal
44 Word of approval
45 "____ d'arte" (Tosca aria)
46 Enrichment course
50 Jiffy
51 Ernani, for one
54 Scand. land
55 Suffix with expert
56 A diva may have a big one
57 Kicker's prop
59 Bathroom fixture
61 Opera performed more than 1,200 times at the Met
64 Opera legend played by Mario Lanza in a 1951 movie
67 The Merry Widow, e.g.
68 Draw in
69 Fuse
70 V-J Day pres.
71 Ticks off

Down

1 ____-Mart
2 Actor Vigoda
3 "King of the high C's"
4 Aida chorus subject
5 Capable of being stretched
6 Brainstorm
7 Upscale hotel amenity
8 Inmates
9 Slothful
10 Part of H.M.S.
11 "____ Dream" (Lohengrin aria)
12 How most arias are sung

Answer on page 88

13 64-Across, notably
16 Battlers, at times
20 Wealthy matron in *Falstaff*
23 Fricka's husband, in the *Ring* cycle
24 Greet the day
27 Pong creator
30 "Bravo!"
31 Summer Games assn.
33 Like a sleeping bag
36 Average vocal range ... or a software app developed by the Met
37 Stops for dates?
38 First African-American to sing multiple leading roles at the Met

40 Upper canines
41 _____ room
45 Green
47 Loose-limbed
48 Schubert's *Symphony No. 8* _____ *Minor*
49 13-Down et al.
51 Not on deck
52 Visibly shocked
53 Prestigious prize
58 CPR givers
60 One-named artist
62 Statute: Abbr.
63 Chow down
65 Actor Rockwell
66 Photo finish?

Next!

This wife of an English king was beautiful, ambitious, and doomed: a bad combination for her, but a great recipe for opera.

Across
1 "Darn it!"
5 Planning detail
9 *Dynasty* actress Linda
14 Privy to
15 Architect Saarinen
16 Where 18-Across premiered (1830)
17 Choice answer?
18 2011–12 season opener at the Met
20 Kind of wave
21 Enough, to Juan
22 Spring
23 One of four, in *Otello*
24 Walk away, in a way
25 You might get steamed here
27 Miniature model
29 _____ *Fledermaus* (Johann Strauss operetta)
30 Windy City team
33 Act 1 setting of 18-Across
37 Upper echelon
39 "Bravo!"
40 A lot
41 Giovanna, in 18-Across
44 Correct ending?
45 Director Howard
46 Tenor Badà, with more than 2,000 Met performances

49 URL ending
50 *Fear of Flying* author
52 Grumpy companion?
53 "_____ she blows!"
56 Take _____ for the worse
58 Peak in les Alpes
59 18-Across, to 2-Down
61 Last part
62 Lord _____, suitor of 18-Across
63 Cupcake topper
64 It may be pumped
65 February forecast
66 Modernists
67 Ain't correct?

Down
1 Tries to strike
2 King in 18-Across
3 Like some elections
4 Cap site
5 Albatross, for one
6 Kind of code
7 Surrealist Max
8 Paint layer
9 Offshoot of punk rock
10 Rome home
11 Protected, at sea
12 Zola heroine
13 Lose it
19 No-frills
24 Rio de _____

Answer on page 90

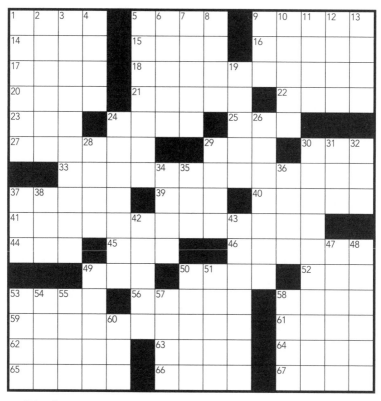

26 Ringing
28 Lincoln or Madison
29 Mendelssohn's "crowd"?
30 Broadway hangouts
31 Obsolete
32 Crosses (out)
34 Planted
35 Suffix with plug
36 Noted work?
37 Footballer Manning
38 John
42 Wanderer
43 Leather workers

47 Act 2 setting of
   18-Across
48 Piece of the pie?
49 "Time in a Bottle" singer
50 Result of squeezing?
51 Gluck operatic title role
53 Cookbook amts.
54 Stiletto, e.g.
55 Fair-sized plot
57 Like some beds
58 1102 on a monument
60 Where Met opera
   reviews appear: Abbr.

Title Game

What's in a name? More than you might realize, in the operatic repertory.

Answer on page 92

Across

1 Some opera singers
6 Mascagni opera, for short
9 Show place?
14 Like some pre-Columbian art
15 Like
16 Perfume name
17 Union member
18 Workers hired for October and November?
20 "Evil Woman" musical gp.
21 *Dido and* _____ (Purcell opera)
22 Musical Reed
23 Log-on need
25 Three, to Tosca
26 Govt. auditors
27 Speck on an Italian city map?
30 The world, according to Shakespeare
32 Harvest goddess
33 Nut jobs
35 Flat
36 TV's Doogie after a day at the beach?
39 Rubberneck
42 Charger
43 Galley propeller
46 Colorful ring
49 Person who often takes care of a baby girl?
51 Env. contents
52 It's inflatable
54 Reproductive cell
55 Suffix with bass
56 Period of legal minority
59 For
60 Actress's smile at a photo shoot?
62 They hold your horses
64 Foe
65 Follower of harvard.
66 One of the Muppets
67 Fiends
68 Start of a *Ring* opera title
69 Engendered

Down

1 "Encore!"
2 Increases the pot
3 Tackle box items
4 Zen enlightenment
5 Hero's end?
6 Momus, in *La Bohème*
7 Bass-baritone Held
8 Figaro, in *Le Nozze di Figaro*
9 Hardy girl and namesakes
10 Pres. when Roberta Peters made her Met debut
11 Like many operas
12 Make new alliances

13 Rendered harmless
19 Zhivago's love
21 Extra
23 _____-Aztecan language
24 On the West Coast, maybe
28 Baron in *Der Rosenkavalier*
29 _____ fairy
31 Rocky point
34 _____'Pea
36 Bout stopper
37 Conductor Koussevitzky
38 Mystery writer Buchanan
39 Telescope pioneer
40 Recital piece
41 Massenet opera

43 Big Apple Circus feature
44 Gardener in *Le Nozze di Figaro*
45 Certain whiskey
47 Bernstein, familiarly, and others
48 Totally wowed
50 Current measure
53 When some turns are allowed
57 Slave girl of opera
58 African herd
61 Soul: French
62 Fighter in gray
63 Opera stage design

Into the Woods

A classic children's tale becomes even more wonderful (and more disturbing) in its operatic incarnation.

Across
1 Singer McEntire
5 Starbuck's captain
9 Round dance
14 Patisserie employee
15 José Carreras calls it home
16 "... and ____ grow on"
17 Time when 37-Across is often performed
19 Studio sign
20 Big bike
21 Composer of 37-Across
23 Reproduce
24 Check out
25 Family that co-founded the Met
28 Inspiration source
30 Part of an opera costume
33 Meditate (on)
34 Grammy winner Twain
36 Novelist Levin
37 English title of an opera that premiered in Weimar in 1893
40 Funny Philips
41 Pamper
42 Bad marks?
43 ____ *Fliegende Holländer* (Wagner opera)
44 Is in the red
45 Grateful?
46 Suffix with meth-

47 Radioed, e.g.
49 Housing material in 37-Across
54 Like Méphistophélès, in *Faust*
57 Video games pioneer
58 Source of 37-Across
60 Carpenter's tool
61 *Alfred* composer
62 "¿Cómo ____ usted?"
63 Staggering
64 Start of something new
65 From

Down
1 Opulent
2 Parrot
3 *Wozzeck* composer
4 Agent Gold of *Entourage*
5 Misbehave
6 Overacting
7 "Rush!"
8 Politician's core support
9 Firestone rival
10 Musical with the song "N.Y.C."
11 Low in fat
12 Narc tail?
13 ____ barrel legislation
18 Restaurateur Toots
22 Quit
23 Bossy types?

Answer on page 94

25 Hurt

26 Humiliate

27 Vocal range of the 30-Down, occasionally

28 Long tresses

29 Ruin

30 Rosine, in 37-Across

31 Princess in Handel's *Tamerlano*

32 Lots of laughter

34 Ritardando, in music

35 Find awful

38 *Modern Family* actor

39 Orient

45 Hardy boy of movies

46 Feel the same

47 Site of two famous banks

48 Dog-____

49 Big Met performance

50 Road to old Rome

51 Basilica center

52 Painters' degs.

53 Like some books

54 Low pitch?

55 Kind of sax

56 Refusing to listen

59 Pekoe, e.g.

Secret Operas

For the answers to these clues, look within.

Across

1 Journal
4 Ballet ____ de Monte Carlo
9 They can be split
14 Italian article
15 Moth-____
16 Donizetti's tragic title character
17 Part of T.G.I.F.
18 Prepared specs a certain way
20 Adds power to, with "up"
22 Extra benefit
23 Group in *Mississippi Burning*
24 Autumn beverage
26 Lacking
27 Bring home
28 Drum site
30 "Ah, Tanya, Tanya," e.g.
33 Baseball's Mel
35 ____ profundo
40 Praised, in a way
44 Checker's move?
45 Half of a 1955 merger
46 "____ well"
47 Mousehawk
50 Survey map
52 Author Janowitz
56 Public meeting place
61 Group of Israeli bankers?

62 Knocks off
63 *Dallas* Miss
64 It's no biggie
67 High rails
68 Make up
69 1545 council site
70 Stout
71 30-Acrosses, e.g.
72 Emma ____, early soprano at the Met
73 Cobb and Burrell

Down

1 ____ *Miller* (Verdi opera)
2 Leading the field
3 Fill the tank
4 Biblical locale
5 Bygone Mideast gp.
6 Fill, as shoes
7 Put in stitches
8 Big course
9 Capp and Capone
10 Plastic surgeons' work
11 City NW of Orlando
12 Italian opera hub
13 Composer Camille Saint-____
19 Gumbo ingredient
21 Begs
25 Riverbank critter
29 Stat for Albert Pujols
30 Befitting

Answer on page 87

31 Undeveloped
32 Sequel's sequel
34 HBO alternative
36 Old explosive
37 French seasoning
38 Big inits. in TV comedy
39 N.B.A. tiebreakers
41 ____ Z
42 Smoker's mouthpiece
43 Veg out
48 Idle fancy
49 Pinpoint

51 Heads-up notices
52 Opera motifs
53 Justice Samuel
54 Opera with the aria
   "Adieu, notre petite table"
55 Word with sing or string
57 Aquarium fish
58 Sheep's peep
59 Budd at the Met
60 Approvals
65 Domicile: Abbr.
66 Compass heading

Murder, She Said

The supremely ambitious wife of the stage becomes even more dangerous and disturbing with music by 15-Across/25-Down.

Across
1 Light carriage
7 Bend shape
10 Dodge
14 Flowering shrub
15 With 25-Down, composer of *Macbeth*
17 Like some stops
18 *Macbeth* extra
19 "____ Little Tenderness"
20 Chair-back material
22 NASA vehicle
23 "Agnus ____"
24 Excites
29 That, in Tijuana
30 Tennis star Gibson
33 Duke Gottfried's sister in *Lohengrin*
34 *CSI* airer
36 ¹/₁₀₀ of a euro
37 Rod's partner
38 Cake with a kick
40 Title for Macbeth
41 Skin: Suffix
42 Gathering clouds, e.g.
43 Stravinsky's *The ____ of Spring*
44 Bit of advice
45 Drill gp.
46 Takes off a bowler
48 Used to be
51 On land

53 Diva's opening?
54 Lob's path
55 Consume
58 Kind of clef
59 *Macbeth* setting
63 Take a chance
65 Macduff, for one
66 Bear witness
67 Ear-related
68 Theta preceder
69 Loved by

Down
1 Act 2 setting of *Macbeth*
2 Blue hues
3 See 26-Down
4 Frances ____, who sang at the Met with Caruso
5 Witness
6 Title role in a German opera
7 Even, to Yves
8 Edelstein of *House*
9 Purify ceremonially
10 Theater/opera director McAnuff
11 Increases
12 Cost-of-living meas.
13 Barbie's fiancé
16 MS accompanier
21 Contribute
23 Court figs.

Answer on page 89

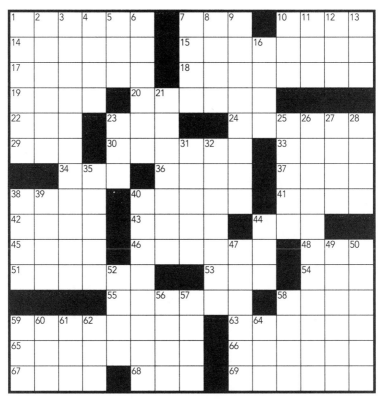

25 See 15-Across
26 3-Down, notably
27 PC person
28 Oil producer
31 Act 1 scene in *Macbeth*
32 Nonets
35 *Macbeth* general whose ghost appears in Act 2
38 When repeated, a getaway island
39 Singer Tori
40 Identity at birth
44 Philosopher Lao-____
47 Foursome

49 Met singer, e.g.
50 Soprano Renata, a memorable 3-Down
52 Rub the wrong way
56 Swarm member
57 Dame ____ Everage
58 Hammett pooch
59 ____-Cat
60 Camp bed
61 *Madama Butterfly* costume feature
62 Pampering, for short
64 East end of Manhattan?

What's My Line?

Even opera characters have to earn a living.

Across

1 Egyptian cobra
4 With 55-Down, longtime Met bass-baritone
9 The _____ Bride (Rimsky-Korsakov opera)
14 _____-jongg
15 L'Elisir d'_____
16 The "O" in OWN
17 Shapiro of NPR
18 Pinkerton, in Madama Butterfly
20 Soup cracker
22 Hairpiece
23 "Fire away!"
24 Humane org.
27 The final say?
31 States
33 Haitian exile of 2004
35 Not relevant
37 Dry runs
39 Oedipus _____ (Stravinsky opera)
40 Summit in Valais
41 Suggestion
42 August hrs.
43 Med. research group
44 Pleases, and more
45 Don Carlo has four (or sometimes five)
46 Make too much of
48 Olympian Lipinski

50 Role in Handel's Agrippina
51 Taximeter reading
53 Soprano Lehmann
56 Wahine's offering
58 Positions
60 Escamillo, in Carmen
65 Porkpie, say
66 In progress
67 High-rise support
68 Suffix with journal
69 Some crossword entries
70 Opera followers?
71 Legal matter

Down

1 Pile up
2 Conductor Caldwell
3 Dr. Faust, in Faust
4 Balance
5 Single-named supermodel
6 Gets going
7 Le Comte _____ (Rossini opera)
8 Opposite of paleo-
9 Protein source
10 Water source
11 Kind of welder
12 Norma _____
13 Nasdaq unit: Abbr.
19 Least sturdy

Answer on page 91

21 Precisely
25 Marcello, in *La Bohème*
26 Jalopy
28 Papageno, in
   The Magic Flute
29 In other words
30 Librettos
32 Early Norwegian king,
   son of Harald
34 Ukraine, once: Abbr.
35 Opera based on a
   Prévost novel
36 Drink garnish
38 Calf catcher
41 _____ diem

45 Tenor in a Schoenberg
   opera
47 Deodorant option
49 Frightens
52 First name in cosmetics
54 Josh
55 See 4-Across
57 Young newts
59 Rush
60 Rotten
61 Saucer, maybe
62 Like bass voices
63 Band booking
64 *Boardwalk Empire*
   broadcaster

Pardon My French

There is something irresistible about flirty French girls—all of whom seem to embody opera's ultimate coquette.

Across

1 Not all there
8 Facet
14 Don Giovanni, say
15 Counter
17 Opera premiere of 1805
18 King who reigned during Prévost's *Manon*
19 Charge
20 Groundskeeper's supply
22 Applesauce brand
23 Retired, maybe
26 With 21-Down, father of Manon's lover
29 Very red celestial bodies
31 All there
32 Stoolie
35 Poker champ Ungar
36 Summer pest
37 Barracks boss, briefly
38 Clone
41 Where *Manon* premiered (1884)
43 Regarding
44 "Double Fantasy" singer
45 Composer often called the inventor of opera
46 "Yada yada yada"
48 Prefix with liberal
49 1813 battle site
50 Duty
54 Manon's surname

57 Category
58 It's a plus
60 Losing line in a game
62 Solo in space
63 Elderly libertine in *Manon*
66 London's Broadway
69 Turns in
70 Good way to live
71 Exodus crossing
72 Old bank giveaway

Down

1 Canada's ____ Island
2 *Manon* setting in 33-/39-Down
3 Feature of some balance sheets
4 "Right you ____!"
5 Zero
6 Seller's sign
7 Seat at the bar
8 Bermuda is in it: Abbr.
9 ____ Tomé
10 Drop sharply
11 *Middlemarch* author
12 Reservoirs
13 Send via cell phone
16 Vacation wheels: Abbr.
21 William ____ (Manon's lover)
24 No trouble
25 Richard Gere title role

Answer on page 93

27 Child's question
28 Working in Hollywood, maybe
30 Trumpeter's high note
33 With 39-Down, start of *Manon*
34 Overly
38 Bamboozle
39 See 33-Down
40 Place to lounge
42 "E lucevan le stelle," e.g.
43 Big lot
45 Apothecary tools

47 Put out
51 Like some cats
52 Massenet's home
53 ____ bender
55 Sniggled
56 Namely
58 Cabinet dept.
59 Plaintiff
61 Prefix with phobia
64 Cockney's residence
65 Airport org.
67 Hot tub
68 Your: French

Looking for the Met

How do you get to the Met? You could practice, or you could look closely through this puzzle.

Across

1 Circus prop
6 What you can find 11 other times in this puzzle's completed grid, looking up, down, backwards, and diagonally, word-search style
9 Take ____ (travel)
14 Home run, slangily
15 Cheer
16 Rodeo rope: Var.
17 Wipe
18 When each Met season usually begins
20 Site of opera's Manoel Theatre
21 Ness and others
22 Goals
23 Itin. part
25 Where 20-Across is: Abbr.
27 Ford's first minivan
32 Tribal emblem
36 *Master Class*, for one
37 Transport for the short haul
39 Massenet opera
41 Gounod opera inspired by Shakespeare
44 Like hedgehogs
45 Mideast capital
46 Trillion: Prefix
47 Mississippi quartet?

49 More honest
51 Axle, e.g.
53 Slippery ____
54 Concerned with
58 Light producer
61 Left at sea?
65 Composer whose only opera was *Fidelio*
67 Soprano Fleming
68 Hard wear?
69 1995 trial name
70 Turkish Empire founder
71 It's good to know them
72 Pro ____ (for now)
73 Recipe parts

Down

1 Brain ____
2 Fictional plantation
3 From Bellini's country: Abbr.
4 Berlioz opera based on *The Aeneid*
5 Foots the bill
6 Lion's share
7 Certain school: Abbr.
8 Home of the brave
9 Exist
10 Puccini melody, e.g.
11 Physics Nobelist Isidor ____
12 Hot pair

Answer on page 95

13 They're expected on fairways
19 Letter-shaped fastener
24 Suffix with launder
26 French roast
27 Loan figs.
28 Skip the formalities?
29 *Groundhog Day* director Harold
30 Newspaper section covering opera
31 Punjabi princes
33 Work on which the Met's *The Enchanted Island* is partly based
34 One in a mess?
35 Bishop's topper
38 Tax-free bond, for short

40 Burn
42 Open court hearing
43 Tollbooth access
48 Aria, usually
50 Some cigars
52 Lifeboat support
54 Construction beam
55 *Quo Vadis* role
56 Fill-in
57 Siouan tribe
59 Parcel (out)
60 _____ Penh, Cambodia: Var.
62 Words from one who 5-Down
63 Take in
64 Till stack
66 *48*_____ (1982 movie)

"It Is ... Love!"

Sometimes, losing your head over a woman is more than a colorful metaphor.

Across

1 Director who won six Oscars
6 G.I. address
9 Defeats
14 Broadcasting
15 Slave girl in 53-Across
16 Computer acronym
17 Public officials in 53-Across
19 La ___, where 53-Across premiered (1926)
20 Fritter (away)
21 Classic muscle cars
23 Kind of sleep
24 Baseball's Bando
25 ___ Palace and Gardens (53-Across setting)
28 The Muses and others, e.g.
30 Inadequate
33 Drop off
36 It leaves a gaping hole
37 Obama, at times
39 Russian range
41 Shirt size: Abbr.
43 New York City's ___ Place
44 Dance in ¾ time
46 Burnoose wearer
48 Electees
49 False god in Verdi's *Nabucco*

50 Dressy shoe
53 Puccini opera about a hard-to-get princess
55 Shoot the breeze
58 Took in
60 Hurry-up order
61 Pupils' surroundings
64 See 52-Down
66 Conductor of the 53-Across premiere
68 Plot of land
69 Night spot?
70 "Out of the question"
71 Glad supporters?
72 Conceit
73 Spanish babies

Down

1 Provide for free
2 Diarist Nin
3 Bamboo chewer
4 One of three posed by 53-Across to would-be suitors
5 Landlocked sea
6 "The Greatest"
7 The three ministers in 53-Across
8 Given the heave-ho
9 Operatic villains, often
10 PC key

Answer on page 87

11 Alessandro ____, founder of the Neapolitan school of opera
12 Shower square
13 Musical kingdom
18 Isabella, *por ejemplo*
22 Approximately
26 Whimper
27 [Sigh]
29 Wall St. trading group
31 Tide controller
32 Drops the ball
33 Deaden
34 "Vesti la giubba," e.g.
35 Slender smokes
38 Colleague of Fermi
40 Berg opera
42 Hence
45 "Jabberwocky" start
47 Storage area
51 How few football games end
52 With 64-Across, suitor of 53-Across
54 Whole bunch
56 Like the characters in 53-Across
57 Tubular pasta
58 Opera rarity
59 O'Hara locale
62 Pour
63 Models (for)
65 Air Force V.I.P.
67 ____-Jet (winter vehicle)

57

Kidnapped

There's such a thing as too much parental love, as shown in this tragedy.

Across

1 Victor _____, author of the play on which 17-Across is based
5 Votes (for)
9 Broad scarf
14 Roman general in *Attila*
15 Drudge
16 Successor to Pope Agatho
17 Verdi opera and protagonist
19 Occupied
20 Ticks off
21 Looked impolitely
22 Faust, for one
26 Ivanhoe's creator
27 Caribbean getaway
28 Send off
30 A.M. drinks
32 Where 17-Across premiered (1851)
34 Sharer's word
35 Change of address, briefly
37 Series shortener: Abbr.
38 Bad omen from 59-Across
40 Wave maker
41 Fan sounds
43 Time sheet abbr.
44 Maddalena, to Sparafucile, in 17-Across
47 Jazz gp.?
48 Lulu
50 Funny Martin
51 Field units
53 Safeguarded
55 Ridiculed
57 Flamand or Olivier, in *Capriccio*
58 Best Supporting Actor of 2006
59 Nobleman in 17-Across
64 Opera segment
65 Move like mud
66 "O _____ and Osiris" (aria from *The Magic Flute*)
67 Sponge
68 Aspen rentals
69 "Questa o quella" singer in 17-Across

Down

1 _____ Royal Highness
2 Blazing gun
3 Light rowboat
4 Hugs, in a letter
5 See 29-Down
6 Soprano whose farewell opera at the Met was 17-Across
7 Preschoolers
8 _____-Caps (candy brand)
9 Supreme Court figure
10 One serving six years
11 17-Across, for one

Answer on page 89

12 Seine feeder
13 Drawn
18 Pastel shade
21 Conductors' guides
22 Hero, at times
23 King Idomeneo, for one
24 Like 17-Across
25 Japanese band
26 ____-chef
29 With 5-Down, western
31 Up one's ____ (hidden)
33 Repeated
36 Propelled a shell
39 Samovars
42 Firing

45 Political topic
46 Good name for a cook?
49 Wagner opera
52 Actress Zellweger
54 Fictional boy detective and others
55 Like some pronouns: Abbr.
56 Menace at 40-Across
57 Libretto
59 Calendar pages: Abbr.
60 Completely free
61 Columbus inst.
62 Beat ending
63 Nautical heading

Operatic Quartet

These four great operas are coming to the Met in the 2011–12 season ...

Across

1 She dies with Radamès
5 Legendary soprano Albanese
10 Declines
14 Knight's garb
15 Terse turndown
16 Trot, say
17 Curved molding
18 Composer of *Khovanshchina*, at the Met in 2011–12
20 See 27-Down
21 Pear variety
22 Tenant
23 Cute-button link
25 Finnish architect
27 Britten opera about good and evil on the high seas, at the Met in 2011–12
31 Start of the Bay State's motto
34 Singer Paul
35 Met expectations?
37 Rte. suggester
39 Tawny cats
41 Senses
43 Wine and cassis drink
44 Labored
46 Lather
47 For fear that

49 Composer of *L'Elisir d'Amore*, at the Met in 2011–12
51 Busy places
53 Slalom section
54 Marked down
57 Family _____
60 Neighbor of Ga.
63 Glass opera inspired by Gandhi's life, at the Met in 2011–12
65 Beef alternative
66 Looked at
67 CBS, e.g.
68 Still competing
69 "... even _____ speak"
70 Méphistophélès, in *Faust*
71 Regarding

Down

1 "Mentre dormi, _____ fomenti" (*L'Olimpiade* aria)
2 *Otello* villain
3 Second opera in the *Ring* cycle
4 Bass, maybe
5 Prom rental
6 Heavily monitored hosp. areas
7 Washington's _____ Range
8 Favored group
9 Bikini, for one

Answer on page 91

10 Spurs
11 Opera's Don Pasquale, e.g.
12 Two-wheeler
13 Ocular woe
19 Check over
21 Dark horse
24 Smelter's residue
26 Oscar winner Brody
27 With 20-Across, distant view at the opera
28 How tuna is packed
29 Brooklyn, informally
30 Positive aspect
32 *Samson et Dalila* composer
33 Absorb a loss
36 Me, myself, ____

38 Italian wine area
40 Verdi opera
42 Consumes
45 Calligraphy, so they say
48 Brett Halliday detective Michael ____
50 The last of 26
52 Mecca for high rollers
54 Greek peak
55 Dundee denials
56 Mulligan, say
58 Hera's mother
59 Have coming
61 Café au ____
62 Countertenor
64 Small inlet
65 Itinerary word

Operatic Quintet

... and these five are, too!

Across

1 Combustible heap
5 Horoscope
10 Contended (for)
14 Flock-related
15 Broadcaster
16 Opera starter
17 Pastiche opera, at the Met in 2011–12, with *The*
20 Ancient
21 Almaviva, in *Il Barbiere di Siviglia*
22 *Casablanca* role
24 Blast from the past
25 Composer of *The Makropulos Case*, at the Met in 2011–12
29 L'Incredibile, in *Andrea Chénier*
31 Put one's two cents in
32 Markers
34 Reader's aid
38 Made rhapsodic
39 Composer of *Ernani*, at the Met in 2011–12
40 Title role for Peter Fonda
41 Old flames
42 Side by side?
43 Yanks and A's, e.g.
44 Price abbr.
45 Biblical opera, at the Met in 2011–12

47 Kind of game?
51 _____ *18* (Uris novel)
52 Title role in a Gluck opera
55 Summer cooler
60 Opera broadcast to movie theaters in 2008, at the Met in 2011–12, with *La*
62 "Uh-huh"
63 Item with pedals
64 "Sempre libera," e.g.
65 Colors for hot weather
66 Prurient looks
67 Understands

Down

1 _____ bargaining
2 Yin's counterpart
3 Lyricist of the musical *Aida*
4 Audio effect
5 What Mimi holds, in Act 1 of *La Bohème*
6 Sellout
7 Fight site
8 Fix up
9 Chi-town daily
10 Dandini, in *La Cenerentola*
11 Start of a famous boast
12 Lab burners
13 Failed to act
18 Wealthy matron in *Falstaff*
19 Do in
23 St. Moritz sights

Answer on page 93

25 Tenor Carreras
26 Pinnacle
27 Good diving score
28 Symbols of industry
29 Khartoum native
30 Letter after chi
33 Vein contents
34 Operatic character whose second husband is the Painter
35 Tina's *30 Rock* co-star
36 Ford product, briefly
37 Capital of Colombia?
39 Dyer's need
43 Old counters

44 Relinquish
46 Straightens
47 Seem appropriate for
48 Early Met diva Tetrazzini
49 "Over the Rainbow" composer
50 Some credit card rewards
51 Get together
53 Fan fave
54 Fix
56 *Slate*, e.g.
57 Debussy's father?
58 Taking care of things
59 Some fund-raisers: Abbr.
61 Serving of corn

Getting Even

This intense and tuneful melodrama was called "the opera that stands for all opera" by a Boston music journal.

Across

1 Trucker's place
4 Minstrel who loves 66-Across
11 Balanchine, to his students
14 Abbr. on a musical score
15 Awakening
16 Show
17 Ipanema locale
18 Rival of 4-Across
20 Don Giovanni, e.g.
22 Arles article
23 1992 Richard Tucker Award winner
24 Makes
26 Sawbuck halves
28 Like some roofs
30 Teaches, with "up"
34 *Les _____-Unis*
35 Swedish import
36 "Sure thing"
37 Marx Brothers movie that featured a performance of 57-Across, with *A*
41 Salute in stanzas
42 Item in a movie vault
43 Pope after John X
44 Opposed
47 Intensify
48 E-mailed a dupe to
49 90° from *norte*

50 Opera composer Carl Maria von _____
53 Palindromic girl's name
54 *The Neverending Story* author Michael
57 Verdi opera about a gypsy woman's revenge
61 It. is there
62 "Voi _____ sapete" (Mozart standard)
63 Party to a certain suit
64 Quick rule?
65 Many wedding guests
66 Heroine of 57-Across
67 Road caution

Down

1 *The Alienist* author
2 57-Across's "Stride la vampa," e.g.
3 Stock companies?
4 Bucko
5 Approximately
6 Ball and chain, say
7 Ancient letter
8 Ideal ending?
9 Don Giovanni, e.g.
10 Best Picture of 1968
11 Lanai neighbor
12 Group of operas that includes *Götterdämmerung*
13 Sitter's headache

Answer on page 95

19 At sea
21 Third of eight
25 Musical pause
26 Boy in a Menotti opera
27 Naif
28 4-Across, vocally
29 "... _____ in the affairs of men": Shakespeare
30 Made content
31 Sudden revelations
32 Chutzpah
33 Setting of 57-Across
35 Jouster's mount
38 Michelangelo's work
39 Shouts for toreadors

40 Former QB Rodney _____
45 Hit man
46 Torah, e.g.
47 More precious
49 Convex molding
50 Cigarette lighter part
51 K-12
52 Bingo call
53 Egyptian sun god: Var.
55 Event in 57-Across
56 So
58 Compete
59 Blood-type letters
60 Pitcher's stat

Taking Back the Throne

A wronged woman makes for a compelling story anywhere, but especially at the opera.

Across

1 Set upon
6 Area meas.
10 Movie cartoon with the voice of Woody Allen
14 Quickly
15 Wheels
16 Its banks are Swiss
17 More refined
18 Buying and selling
20 ____ *Freischütz* (Weber opera)
21 Met title role for Renée Fleming
23 Friendly intro?
24 *Hansel and Gretel* prop
25 Plant anew
28 Actor Cariou
29 Send another way
32 Suffix with orange
33 Map abbr. until 1991
34 It has many keys: Abbr.
35 Nordic runners
36 German bass René
39 Setting of 21-Across
41 "Warm" or "warmer"
42 Kind of movie screen
43 Kerfuffle
44 Watchdog's warning
46 Climax
47 Distance of some races
49 Unstinting amount

52 Desolate
54 Gusted
55 Scare word
56 Machiavellian character in 21-Across
59 Longtime Met singer Vickers
60 Refrigerator attachments
62 Golf outing
64 Pride of lions?
65 *Momo* writer Michael
66 1997 Literature Nobelist Fo
67 Stratagem
68 Eye sore
69 Dutch genre painter

Down

1 Composer of 21-Across
2 Per
3 Synthetic fabric
4 Bridge topper?
5 Real 60-Downs
6 Not so sunny
7 21-Across's title
8 Verdi's lang.
9 ____ me tangere
10 Cable choice
11 *Madama Butterfly* setting
12 Numerical prefix
13 Road to enlightenment
19 Memo header

Answer on page 87

22 Provide excess staffing
26 Wotan, in Norse myth
27 *La Fanciulla del* ____
   (Puccini opera)
30 Suffix with form
31 Movie based on the story
   of Rapunzel
33 Census category
35 Stk. unit
36 Snaps
37 Latin 101 verb
38 Comedic role in *The Magic
   Flute*
40 Chemical ending

45 Paraphrases
47 Pod holder
48 "Maybe"
49 Repudiate
50 Canadian dollar,
   informally
51 Where 21-Across premiered
   (1725)
53 Met bass Samuel
57 Alibi ____ (excuse makers)
58 Inclination
60 Little dickens
61 Baseball's Ripken
63 Stable particle?

The Competition

Not all the drama is *on* the stage in the opera world. Vying to get to the Met stage is a truly operatic journey for young singers in the prestigious National Council Auditions.

Across

1 Cleopatra's last bite?
4 Totters
9 Check mates?
14 Keep out
15 Eagerly accept
16 Callas who taught at Juilliard
17 Buddy
18 A winner of the 1958 National Council Auditions
20 Sturdy, in a way
22 Roth ____
23 Super Bowl highlights?
24 A winner of the 1981 National Council Auditions
29 Manuscript sheet
30 Up to
31 *Rocky* ____
33 Things to chew on
36 Shone intensely
40 A winner of the 1994 National Council Auditions
44 With 45-Across, Tinseltown transaction
45 See 44-Across
46 Tee preceder
47 Whiz
49 Discrimination

52 A winner of the 1961 National Council Auditions
57 Mellow
59 It may be radical
60 Paris underground
61 A winner of the 1988 National Council Auditions
66 Empty (of)
67 Preface
68 Where Massenet studied
69 Superlative
70 Mean mien
71 Be in control
72 Buddy

Down

1 Prior's superior
2 Vaughan of jazz
3 Composer of *The Fiery Angel*
4 Royalty-related
5 Conductor's need
6 J.F.K. posting
7 Notable Met role for Lily Pons
8 Kind of whale
9 Dallas sch.
10 Tufted topper
11 ____ sprawl
12 Flier

Answer on page 89

13 Reveals
19 Bill Clinton, for one: Abbr.
21 Rock type
25 Director Vittorio De _____
26 Pester
27 Place for a houseplant
28 Oil of _____
31 Doctrine
32 Skater Midori
34 _____ Frau ohne Schatten (Richard Strauss opera)
35 The Met has about 3,800
37 Some minds, in a comparison
38 Quizzical sounds
39 Wagner's Der Ring _____ Nibelungen
41 Snowman's prop
42 Operatic tenor, often
43 Bor-r-ring
48 Not a copy: Abbr.
50 Stew
51 Torino trio
52 Beau _____
53 Pierces
54 Pass
55 Novelist Jong
56 Peak performance?
57 "No returns"
58 Title baritone in the Met's 2011–12 Billy Budd
62 It may come after you
63 Eur. monarchy
64 Ground breaker
65 Bar choice

Olé!

Opera's ultimate bad girl maintains as tight a grip on audiences as she does on every man who crosses her path.

Across

1 Square
7 Have trouble with sisters?
11 "Vieni, amor ____" (*Madama Butterfly* aria)
14 These days
15 Man chaser?
16 Canine care org.
17 "____ Song" (aria sung by 30-Down)
18 "____ Song" (aria sung by 49-Across)
20 One-third of *Capriccio*?
22 Part of N.F.L.
23 Long stories
26 Like 60-Across
31 Weizman of Israel
32 Long ____
33 Sister of Clio
34 Some campers
35 Good sense
38 Place to hibernate
39 Percent add-on
40 Frights
41 #6 of Sixers fame
42 Reason for another serve
43 Categorize
44 ____-Japanese
45 Hidey-holes
47 Some officers: Abbr.
48 After-dinner selection
49 18-Across, in 60-Across

52 Swiss city, old-style
53 Henry VIII's third
54 Klinger portrayer
56 Aria sung by 60-Across
60 Bizet opera about a gypsy who lives for the moment
64 See 65-Across
65 With 64-Across, primitive time
66 Extremely
67 Impresario Hurok
68 Squabbling
69 Opera's Scarpia, e.g.

Down

1 Little one
2 Actor Kilmer
3 WWII inits.
4 Dealer's delivery
5 ____ *Gold* (1997 movie)
6 Norma's fate, in *Norma*
7 Shooting site
8 "Forget it!"
9 One of the Churchills
10 Little Leaguers, e.g.
11 Lucia's "____ Scene"
12 Prelude to a kiss?
13 Implement with a collar
19 Bygone spray
21 Blacksmiths
23 60-Across setting

Answer on page 91

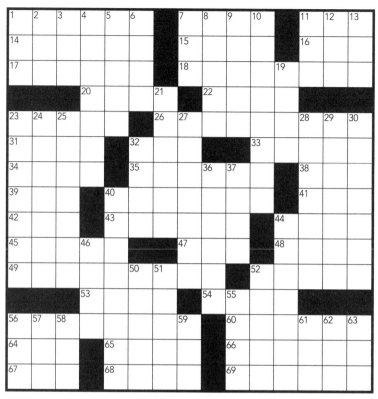

24 Spring bloomers
25 Kind of code
27 Doing really well
28 Pops
29 Endless
30 Suitor of 60-Across
32 Very, in Versailles
36 Somewhat
37 Scraps
40 Hobart's land
44 Sang 60-Across, say
46 Big Indian

50 Static
51 _____ de Lahore (Massenet opera)
52 Cheer at the Met
55 Ones on the links?
56 Orders
57 Long _____
58 _____ canto
59 Caste member
61 Dr.'s order
62 Twisty curve
63 "Just the opposite!"

Figaro's Day of Madness

A lot can happen in one day, but a smart servant's marriage assures that all will live happily ever after ... or will they?

Across

1 Heart
5 Important mo. at the Met
8 Composer of *Le Nozze di Figaro*
14 Three digits before seven
16 Ready to run
17 Ceremony during Figaro's "Day of Madness"
18 "Haven't heard anything yet"
19 Nice time?
20 Famous part of *Le Nozze di Figaro*
22 Parent
24 I-90 runs through this city
25 *Die Walküre*, e.g.
29 Put in
31 Sonoma neighbor
34 Goose egg
35 Chop _____
38 Figaro's bride
40 Lorenzo _____, *Le Nozze di Figaro* librettist
43 Royal in *Die Frau ohne Schatten*
44 Oscar-winning movie about 8-Across
45 Retreat
46 Me, to Mimi
47 Fool
49 Gives a free pass

53 Gets it wrong
55 Aviation-related
58 Contemptible one
59 With 67-Across, *Le Nozze di Figaro* role
63 Little dipper?
64 Fleming and Netrebko, at times
67 See 59-Across
69 Literally, "high ground"
70 Was stranded, in a way
71 Where *Le Nozze di Figaro* premiered (1786)
72 Alto, for countertenor: Abbr.
73 Costner role

Down

1 Shooter
2 Gave a stem-winder
3 Check, maybe
4 Musical sense
5 "Sull'aria ... che _____ zeffiretto"
6 Gadget for a lawn job
7 Look through a keyhole
8 PC pop-up
9 It's in the dumps
10 Fan mags
11 Nibbled away
12 VCR button
13 Tom Brady stats

Answer on page 93

15 A.F.L.'s partner
21 Prickly plant
23 Do a lawn job
26 _____ Brown, the original
   Bess in *Porgy and Bess*
27 Goes out?
28 "Too bad"
30 Beach views
32 Reebok rival
33 Kind of jelly
36 Travel bag item
37 Toady
39 Hood's projectile
40 Kiri Te Kanawa, e.g.
41 Bow and 39-Down user
42 Duet
48 Bees' spots

50 Sleuth's discovery
51 Bears out
52 Impugns
54 Show disdain for
56 Track event
57 Overseer in Mozart's
   *The Abduction from the
   Seraglio*
60 _____ even keel
61 Andy Roddick's gp.
62 Elegiac
64 Big D hoopster
65 Actress Meyers
66 Rebuff from Macduff
68 *Die Meistersinger
   _____ Nürnberg*
   (Wagner opera)

Going Solo

For all the grandeur of opera, the most exciting moments often feature one great singer alone on the stage.

Across
1 Times in classifieds
4 *Un Ballo in Maschera* highlight
9 Bundles
14 Greek cross
15 Attack
16 Functional
17 Get ready for war
18 Famous aria in *Turandot*
20 Doddered
22 Poach
23 Roué's look
24 Boomers' kids
25 C.S.A. general
28 Debark
34 Welcome sight?
36 Cuba, por ejemplo
38 High land
39 Famous aria in *Gianni Schicchi*
43 First lady of the 1950s
44 Scott Turow title
45 Job for AAA
46 Like many operatic performances
49 Fab Four name
51 Flair
53 Drops in the air
56 Unsuccessful, as a mission
61 Elvira's love, in a Verdi opera

63 Famous aria sung by Radamès
65 *Live from the* ____ (old PBS series)
66 A chorus line?
67 Ancient Greek
68 Unfavorable
69 About to receive
70 Rosa, in *From Russia With Love*
71 Pintful, maybe

Down
1 In the least
2 Wozzeck's common-law wife, in *Wozzeck*
3 Famous Gershwin aria sung by Clara and Bess
4 Sea eagle
5 Bemoaned
6 Special ties
7 Opposite of kitsch
8 Sudden reversals
9 Chums
10 Surmounting
11 Modena money, once
12 City of ____ (New Haven)
13 Noted septet
19 Boy-door connection
21 Start to date?
24 General manager of the 65-Across since 2006

Answer on page 95

26 Write wrongs?
27 Conductor _____-Pekka Salonen
29 _____ Gay
30 Delt neighbor
31 Famous aria sung by Aida
32 Betting game
33 Course
34 May V.I.P.s
35 Third in a Latin series
37 Typing system?
40 Monet work
41 The 65-Across, for one: Abbr.
42 After discounts
47 Some
48 Unmask

50 Role in a John Adams opera: Abbr.
52 "Fantabulous!"
54 Fishhook line
55 Kind of operatic role
56 When Rinaldo kills Gernando, in Rossini's *Armida*
57 Swiss capital
58 Norway's patron saint
59 Realtor's expertise, for short
60 Ivan IV of opera
61 Touch up, in a way
62 Dash
64 Addams Family member

The Sound of Music

This fairy tale by Mozart is part hero quest, part fantastic voyage, and all pure delight for all ages.

Across

1 Little chow
4 Cable letters
7 Wild cat
13 Intimidate
16 Abducted princess in 25-Across
17 Abductor of 16-Across
18 Best, as friends
19 It may be upped
20 Mid sixth-century year
22 Do nothing
23 "Donde lieta usci" singer
25 Mozart opera featuring 65-Across and 69-Across looking for love, with *The*
29 Apartments, e.g.
31 Soldier at Vicksburg
32 Rodeo performer
33 "____ be my pleasure"
34 It's needed to find the right key
36 Commuter's option
38 *William Tell* composer
40 Took off
44 Like some Met performances
45 "Not nice!"
46 D.C.'s Constitution, e.g.
47 It's a wrap
50 Superlative finish
52 Mountain resort
54 Slave of 17-Across
57 Fleming and others
58 Knack
59 Chiwere speaker
60 10 C-notes
62 Met conductor Fritz
65 See 25-Across
69 See 25-Across
70 Title role in another Mozart opera
71 Places
72 Kirsten Flagstad's country: Abbr.
73 Way back when

Down

1 Letter ender?
2 Olympics chant
3 Location in 25-Across, at times
4 Where heads are put together
5 Nut case
6 Dull plodder
7 Eye-related
8 One for the road
9 It won't fly
10 Is out of commission, as a ship
11 Not remote
12 Shred
14 "Enough already!"

Answer on page 87

15 President when the first Met telecast aired on ABC
21 Opera text
23 Sierra Club founder
24 Grooving on
26 Come to
27 *Das Rheingold* mezzo-soprano
28 Alfio's wife, in *Cavalleria Rusticana*
30 Big fishing nets
35 Social climber?
37 Stubborn sort
39 Song sung singly
41 Whom 65-Across finally loves

42 Uniform
43 Places to listen to opera
47 Street _____
48 Mauled
49 Punctual
51 Drop by
53 *The _____ of Corinth* (Rossini opera)
55 Corrida figures
56 Deep sleep
61 *China Beach* locale
63 Actress Vardalos
64 Close
66 Flurry
67 Photog's item
68 Reset setting

Passing the Baton

The "mission control" center of every performance at the Met, the conductor's podium has hosted a remarkable roster of the most celebrated names in music.

Across

1 Gem State capital
6 Fat cat
11 Bon Jovi, e.g.
14 ____ Seidl, who conducted the opening of the 1885 season
15 Rosalinde's maid in *Die Fledermaus*
16 Five-spot
17 Conductor who made his Met debut in 1942
19 Table-hop
20 Split for the church?
21 Least friendly
23 Lake houses
26 Presides over
27 Jibe
28 Took a course?
30 *The Deep* co-star, 1977
33 In addition
34 Pay a visit to
36 Long, long time
37 *The First Emperor* composer ____ Dun
38 Conductor's title
39 Energy
40 Spanish riches
41 Going to the airport, maybe
42 Contralto Chookasian
43 Say 22-Down again

45 Mental
46 *The Maids* playwright
47 Akron AA baseball team
49 Cantankerous
50 Stimulus
52 Owning land
54 Fate
55 Met conductor whose students included Leonard Bernstein
60 Knock out
61 Coca-Cola brand
62 Benjamin
63 "Civil" event in *I Puritani*
64 Clip
65 Encouraged, with "on"

Down

1 Capture
2 Combined
3 "Was ____ blame?"
4 Raids
5 Pistons' place
6 Graham of rock
7 Wood trimmer
8 Comb maker
9 Hardy, to Stan
10 Beverly Sills specialty
11 Conductor at the Met since 1971
12 Butterfly effects?
13 Right after

Answer on page 89

18 Foreign visitors?
22 Union words
23 Radamès, e.g., in *Aida*
24 Blazing
25 Met conductor who was a protégé of Gustav Mahler
26 The seas, e.g.
28 First-stringers
29 "O dolci mani" opera
31 Slave
32 Ill will
34 Angelo or Antonio starter
35 Wall St. maven
38 Gym rat's focus
42 _____ library
44 Fish in a pot
46 Where Maria Callas received her musical education
48 Big fan of Dr. Oz
49 Bruins skating great
50 Chink in the armor
51 Herbert Hoover's birthplace
52 Lead-in to girl or boy
53 Head honcho
56 Suffix with glass
57 Holiday quaff
58 Summer on the Somme
59 Abashed

A Girl Could Go Crazy

With love and duty pulling at you from opposite sides, sometimes what rips is the veil between sanity and bloody madness.

Across

1 Baseball's Vizquel
5 Some protests
10 Final Four letters
14 Life, to Montserrat Caballé
15 Go further than
16 Messes up
17 Jai ____
18 Western range
19 Genesis son
20 Castle home of 36-Across
22 Fully stretched
23 ____ sauce
24 Conductor's abbr.
25 Newspaper section
26 Bellyacher
29 Get added to the payroll
30 Like a Burns acquaintance
31 Not too impressed
35 Three-layer snack
36 Donizetti title role
37 Wounded Knee site: Abbr.
41 See 41-Down
42 Designer Chanel
43 Vital
47 Things on rings
49 Hall of fame
50 It goes back and forth
53 Stock page letters
54 Buggy
55 Her breakthrough role was 36-Across

59 Not stiff
60 Sacred opera by Anton Rubinstein
61 Realm
62 Forester's concern: Abbr.
63 Law school newbies
64 Cub or Red, briefly
65 Tender
66 Lose it
67 Scale opening

Down

1 Racer's path
2 Kunis of *Black Swan*
3 Water
4 Chaplain who tells 36-Across not to marry Edgardo
5 Number of acts in *Manon Lescaut*
6 Jungian concept
7 Title with a tilde
8 4-Down, to 36-Across
9 Box a bit
10 Empty ____
11 Write an opera, e.g.
12 Victim of 36-Across
13 See 44-Down
21 Observe
25 Start of day or night
26 *Nixon in China* role
27 ____ *Town* (Wilder play)

Answer on page 91

28 Like a legal pad
29 Attends, as a recital
32 Prejean, in *Dead Man Walking*
33 One of three in 36-Across's opera
34 Golf's Michelle
37 20-Across setting
38 Verdi opera about the Infante of Spain
39 Starting pitcher, usually
40 Floors
41 Lincoln 41-Across?
43 Where 36-Across premiered (1835)

44 With 13-Down, brother of 36-Across
45 Charm
46 Golf ball feature
48 A.L. team on scoreboards
50 "Il dolce ____" (36-Across aria)
51 Offshore
52 Young lion
55 E.P.A. concern
56 *In* ____ (existing)
57 Poetic adverb
58 Bell the cat

World Premieres at the Met

Operas don't only appear in repertory at the Met;
several important operas premiered there.

Across

1 Brahms's "____
   Rhapsody"
5 Noggins
11 Flat hat
14 "High Hopes" lyricist
15 Kind of view
16 Online gasp
17 2006 Tan Dun world
   premiere at the Met
20 "Gloria all'Egitto" opera
21 Bobby ____
22 1918 Giacomo Puccini
   world premiere at the Met
27 Yankee nickname
29 Leeds's river
30 Roxy Music co-founder
31 ____ fan tutte
32 Once called
33 With 50-Across, 1991 John
   Corigliano world premiere
   at the Met
37 Bullwinkle, e.g.
38 Table scraps
39 1999 John Harbison
   world premiere at the Met,
   with *The*
43 Home sick
46 Theater/opera director
   Zimmerman
47 Rod
48 Acapulco approval

49 First mate?
50 See 33-Across
53 *Marco Polo Sings* ____
   (John Guare play)
55 Boast
56 2005 Tobias Picker
   world premiere at the Met,
   with *An*
62 Every other hurricane
63 Richard Strauss opera
64 Healing balm
65 Numbskull
66 Stories told in court
67 Card, e.g.

Down

1 There's only one in
   63-Across
2 ____-di-dah
3 Covent Garden, e.g.
4 Passionate
5 Weight in gems
6 Domicile: Abbr.
7 Oil field?
8 Never, in Nuremberg
9 Reply to "You are not!"
10 Dog bowl brand
11 *Carmen* extras
12 Tenderly, to Toscanini
13 Baseball V.I.P.
18 Old dictator's name
19 Demands

Answer on page 93

22 Singer Janis
23 Prevaricate
24 Adolescent
25 Mozart's *Sonata ____ for Keyboard and Violin*
26 Regulars on *The View*, e.g.
28 "What's the ____?"
33 Tad
34 Big pig
35 Ball
36 34-Down's digs
37 *The Magic Flute* director Julie
39 A.M. TV offering, briefly
40 "Morir! Sì pura e bella" singer
41 Lead removers

42 Blacken
43 Result of drilling?
44 Practice
45 Frank McCourt memoir
48 Campaign staple
50 Outspoken
51 Farmland
52 Pension supplement, for short
54 Soprano Saffer
56 "Can't fool me!"
57 Noted ring leader
58 Head, slangily
59 "More than I need to know," informally
60 ____-eyed
61 Suffix with law or saw

Finale

Some of opera's greatest masterpieces have also served as their composers' farewell to both the theater and to us in the audience.

Across
1 Ear dangler
5 Tease
8 Bullfighter
14 Composer Charles
15 Chemical suffix
16 Any of the Magi
17 Verdi's last opera
19 Battle of ____ Bay, 1898
20 Priest of Shiloh
21 Some Surrealist art
23 Scuffling
24 Mozart's last (performed) opera
28 Tempter
30 Dishwasherful
31 Too suave
32 Least perilous
35 Repeated bit in a song
38 Cooler in summer
39 Tchaikovsky's last opera
40 In ____ Shoes (2005 movie)
41 Expand, in a way
42 Sullies
43 See 1-Down
44 Crown
45 Operatic characters
46 Britten's last opera
52 Exchange words?
53 Small dresses
54 Crackerjack
57 Contralto Anderson

60 Puccini's last opera
62 Opera set on Cyprus
63 Do sum work
64 Outdo
65 Six-winged being
66 ____ Contes d'Hoffmann (Offenbach opera)
67 Bernstein's "Glitter and Be Gay," e.g.

Down
1 With 43-Across, Mae West
2 Face shape
3 Disparaged
4 Count concluder?
5 What to do after an errant shot
6 Prefix with structure
7 Cloud up
8 Skye cap
9 ____ Mae (Whoopi's *Ghost* role)
10 1980s White House name
11 Aria that ends with "O speranze d'amor!"
12 Turned back on
13 Stand and deliver
18 Feds
22 ____ partner
25 It's cut and dried
26 Charges

Answer on page 95

27 _____ Morgana (mirage)
28 Kind of opera
29 Its closing duet is "O terra, addio"
32 "Me, too"
33 Ones who are worlds apart
34 Buff
35 Oscar-winning movie for Kate Winslet
36 Breather
37 They may be performing
39 Zinc oxide target
43 Carpet cleaner, briefly
44 Opera first performed at the Met in 2010

45 City with an opera house named for Verdi
46 Some cars
47 Online meeting place
48 Publicist, say
49 Like some signs
50 Radiate
51 Teen types
55 Start of a Mozart opera title
56 Italian suffix meaning "little"
58 Height for Heidi
59 Tokyo stage show
61 Court org.

Moonstruck

```
L E S S O N   B A R S   A M I
A R T U R O   E L E C T R I C
G A R R E T   L A B O H E M E
      S I L L S   O A S I S
M U S E T T A     A P T
A N K L E   S T A G E   A H A
N I E L S   C U B E D   P E C
I T I S   P A R I S   S P A T
N A N   S O L I D   S T A R T
A S S   I N A N E   A L L O W
    O S S   R O D O L F O
I C A N T   P I S A N
M A R C E L L O   R E N T E D
A F T E R Y O U   I S A I A H
X E S   S E T S   N S T A R S
```

Picture This

```
B A S A L   D O I T   C R A B
A R O S E   E R D A   H I D E
L I F E I S B E A U T I F U L
D A T A S E T     I N T E L
      N O R   E M U
W A L L S T R E E T   P E R P
I M A G E   S A N A   R E A
F A T A L A T T R A C T I O N
E R E   L I R A   O U T I E
Y A R D   R A G I N G B U L L
    R A Y   E N E
O S C A R   S A L A M I S
T H E F I F T H E L E M E N T
R E N T   I G O R   A M A T I
A R T S   T I N T   D O N O R
```

Cutting Edge

```
O R I E L S   L E S   I R O N
R E N T A L   A V A   C O M O
F I G A R O   R E D E E M E D
E N O   P A G   L I E N S
O S T A R   R O S S I N I
    L E S C A U T   T I C
E N D I V E   L E E   R A T E
B A R B E R O F S E V I L L E
A M B I   A M A   V I N Y L S
Y E A   P A C K E T S
    R O B E R T A   A E T N A
I N T W O   O L A   R I D
T O O L B E L T   R O S I N A
E L L E   Y O U   P R O T E M
M O O T   E L M   S E D E R S
```

Ring Master

```
S A F E S   M O M   I N A W E
A M O R E   E R I   C A B O T
G I L D A   N O R S E M Y T H
    K A R A T   R A D   S A Y
E L L   A D O   O V O   S N L
B O O   C O *   * O U T
B O R D E *   * T O S S
S T I R             M I A S
  S C A R *     * A B E L L
    G A S *   * E D   G T O
D A S   I T T   T R U   F I B
O D A   D E A   O S L E R
W A G N E R I A N   A R I A S
S M E A R   L I E   T I E T O
E S S E S   S R S   E N D E D
```

* = RING

86

Secret Operas

```
L O G   R U S S E   A T O M S
U N A   E A T E N   L U C I A
I T S   D R E W T O S C A L E
S O U P S   P E R K   K L A N
A P P L E C I D E R   S A N S
    E A R N   E A R
A R I A   O T T   B A S S O
P A I D A C O M P L I M E N T
T W I S T   C I O   A L L S
    O W L   P L A T
T A M A   H O T E L L O B B Y
E L A L   I C E S   E L L I E
M I N O R M A T T E R   E L S
A T O N E   T R E N T   A L E
S O N G S   E A M E S   T Y S
```

"It Is … Love!"

```
C A P R A   A P O   B E S T S
O N A I R   L I U   A S C I I
M A N D A R I N S   S C A L A
P I D D L E   G T O S   R E M
  S A L   I M P E R I A L
  E N N E A D S   L A M E
N A P   Y A W N   O R A T O R
U R A L S   L G E   A S T O R
M I N U E T   A R A B   I N S
B A A L   W I N G T I P
  T U R A N D O T   R A P
A T E   A S A P   I R I S E S
C A L A F   T O S C A N I N I
T R A C T   I N N   I C A N T
V A S E S   E G O   N E N E S
```

Taking Back the Throne

```
H A D A T   S Q I N   A N T Z
A P A C E   A U T O   A A R E
N I C E R   D E A L I N G I N
D E R   R O D E L I N D A
E C O   O V E N   R E S O W
L E N   R E R O U T E   A D E
  S S R   F L A   S K I S
P A P E   M I L A N   H I N T
I M A X   A D O   G R R
C A P   O N E M I L E   A L L
S T A R K   B L E W   B O O
  G A R I B A L D O   J O N
I C E M A K E R S   R O U N D
M A N E   E N D E   D A R I O
P L O Y   S T Y E   S T E E N
```

The Sound of Music

```
P U P   T B S   O C E L O T
P S Y C H O U T   P A M I N A
S A R A S T R O   T R U E S T
  A N T E   D L I   S I T
M I M I   M A G I C F L U T E
U N I T S   R E B   R O P E R
I T D   E A R   R A I L
R O S S I N I   E S C A P E D
  O N T V   T S K   A V E
S T O L E   E S T   A S P E N
M O N O S T A T O S   I A N S
A R T   O T O   O N E G
R E I N E R   P A P A G E N O
T A M I N O   I D O M E N E O
S T E A D S   N O R   A G O
```

Start-Ups

```
C A P S   S A G A S   B I O S
H I L O   U B O A T   E M M A
A M A T   N A T H A N G U N N
R E N T   T S O     O A S I S
D E B O R A H V O I G T
      V A N   E X T S   R O I
C A P O N   T R I O   H E L P
P L A C I D O   D O M I N G O
A L P E   I N G E   O N E A D
S A E   G O G O   S O D
      A N N A N E T R E B K O
T O S C A     E L Y   M O N A
B R Y N T E R F E L   I G O R
S A N E   B O O N E   T I L E
P L E D   B O R I S   H E L D
```

The Fallen Woman

```
L E I   F L A P   P I T I E S
E L S   E I R E   I N A R U T
V I O L E T T A   V A L E R Y
I N L E T   N O O N E
N O D S   C O U R T E S A N S
E R E S   A L T O S   N E E
      O G R E S   T E N O R
A L F R E D O   G E R M O N T
N U R S E   M I M E O
I C E   T H E R M   T A P A
L A T R A V I A T A   I T I S
      E S S E S   N O T E S
V E N I C E   L A F E N I C E
A R E N O T   E Z I O   L E T
T R Y S T S   S O B S   A S S
```

Noteworthy People

Looking Back

Murder, She Said

Kidnapped

The Competition

Passing the Baton

Promises, Promises

Letters from the Big Apple

Let's Make a Deal

Next!

What's My Line?

A	S	P		S	I	M	O	N		T	S	A	R	S
M	A	H		A	M	O	R	E		O	P	R	A	H
A	R	I		N	A	V	Y	O	F	F	I	C	E	R
S	A	L	T	I	N	E			R	U	G			
S	H	O	O	T		S	P	C	A		O	B	I	T
		S	A	Y	S		A	R	I	S	T	I	D	E
M	O	O	T		T	R	I	A	L	S		R	E	X
A	L	P		P	O	I	N	T	E	R		D	S	T
N	I	H		E	L	A	T	E	S		A	C	T	S
O	V	E	R	R	A	T	E			T	A	R	A	
N	E	R	O		F	A	R	E		L	O	T	T	E
		L	E	I			S	T	A	N	C	E	S	
B	U	L	L	F	I	G	H	T	E	R		H	A	T
A	F	O	O	T		I	B	E	A	M		E	S	E
D	O	W	N	S		G	O	E	R	S		R	E	S

Operatic Quartet

A	I	D	A		L	I	C	I	A		E	B	B	S
M	A	I	L		I	C	A	N	T		G	A	I	T
O	G	E	E		M	U	S	S	O	R	G	S	K	Y
R	O	W		B	O	S	C		L	E	S	S	E	E
		A	S	A			A	A	L	T	O			
B	I	L	L	Y	B	U	D	D		E	N	S	E	
A	N	K	A		O	P	E	R	A	S		A	A	A
C	O	U	G	A	R	S		I	N	T	U	I	T	S
K	I	R		T	O	I	L	E	D		S	N	I	T
	L	E	S	T		D	O	N	I	Z	E	T	T	I
			H	I	V	E	S			E	S	S		
O	N	S	A	L	E		T	R	E	E		A	L	A
S	A	T	Y	A	G	R	A	H	A		V	E	A	L
S	E	E	N		A	I	R	E	R		I	N	I	T
A	S	W	E		S	A	T	A	N		A	S	T	O

Olé!

E	V	E	N	U	P		L	I	S	P		M	I	O
L	A	T	E	L	Y		O	W	A	R		A	D	A
F	L	O	W	E	R		T	O	R	E	A	D	O	R
			C	E	E	S		N	A	T	L			
S	A	G	A	S		H	O	T	H	E	A	D	E	D
E	Z	E	R		T	O	N		E	R	A	T	O	
V	A	N	S		R	E	A	S	O	N		D	E	N
I	L	E		T	E	R	R	O	R	S		D	R	J
L	E	T		A	S	S	O	R	T		S	I	N	O
L	A	I	R	S			L	T	S		T	E	A	S
E	S	C	A	M	I	L	L	O		B	A	S	L	E
			J	A	N	E		F	A	R	R			
H	A	B	A	N	E	R	A		C	A	R	M	E	N
A	G	E		I	R	O	N		E	V	E	R	S	O
S	O	L		A	T	I	T		S	A	D	I	S	T

A Girl Could Go Crazy

O	M	A	R		F	A	S	T	S		N	C	A	A
V	I	D	A		O	N	E	U	P		E	R	R	S
A	L	A	I		U	I	N	T	A		S	E	T	H
L	A	M	M	E	R	M	O	O	R		T	A	U	T
			S	O	Y		A	R	R		M	E	T	R	O
M	O	A	N	E	R			H	I	R	E	O	N	
A	U	L	D		U	N	A	W	E	D				
O	R	E	O		L	U	C	I	A		S	D	A	K
			C	E	N	T	E	R			C	O	C	O
N	E	E	D	E	D			S	T	O	N	E	S	
A	N	N	I	E		S	A	W		O	T	C		
P	R	A	M		S	U	T	H	E	R	L	A	N	D
L	I	M	P		M	O	S	E	S		A	R	E	A
E	C	O	L		O	N	E	L	S		N	L	E	R
S	O	R	E		G	O	A	P	E		D	O	R	E

Surname Game

```
LOIS _ ACAR _ SEMIS
OMNI _ ELSA _ TRITE
BERNSTEIN _ ADMIT
ONEGINOFFAGAIN _
_ _ ERA _ _ ODE _ _
FOUR _ CARR _ SPAS
ACT _ ATAD _ IDEATE
THISBUDDSFORYOU
SELLER _ LOTS _ ENS
OREO _ NEED _ _ SEES
_ _ _ SOP _ _ PEC _ _
_ JUSTNOTGODUNOV
POPPY _ CHERUBINI
RATON _ HANG _ ALES
ENOTE _ STAY _ SERA
```

Out of Africa

```
CATERTO _ WIRETAP
EMOTION _ ASARULE
RADAMES _ VISITOR
ERAS _ _ INES _ TONS
SAY _ ASTI _ SURGE _
_ _ _ TOWELBAR _ _ _
NAPOLI _ EURIDICE
ECRU _ VERDI _ ONES
GEORGEVI _ SCENES
_ _ _ ELEVATOR _ _ _
ASKME _ ETON _ SPY
RELO _ AARE _ _ PARE
MEMPHIS _ AMNERIS
ENNEADS _ SEARACE
DOORMAT _ ENGINES
```

Opening Credits

```
FLU _ OPAL _ BARBER
LAFENICE _ ARTURO
IDOMENEO _ SMELLS
PESO _ _ RICHE _ LEA
_ _ _ TABS _ HERB _ _
STPETE _ PARSIFAL
AHI _ ONTAP _ _ NERO
LENOZZEDIFIGARO
MITT _ _ LUNAR _ TAN
ARABELLA _ CENSUS
_ _ _ STEM _ ITSO _ _
BAY _ EPEES _ _ CRAB
AMONRA _ LABOHEME
SIDING _ MASSENET
SEABEE _ SCAT _ TRA
```

Title Game

```
BASSI _ CAV _ THIRD
INCAN _ ALA _ ESTEE
STATE _ FALLSTAFF
_ ELO _ AENEAS _ LOU
USERID _ _ TRE _ IRS
TURINDOT _ ASTAGE
OPS _ LOCOS _ _ ONED
_ _ _ TANHOWSER _ _ _
GAWK _ STEED _ OAR
AREOLA _ HERNANNY
LTR _ EGO _ _ GAMETE
IST _ NONAGE _ PRO _
LOHANGRIN _ REINS
ENEMY _ EDU _ ERNIE
OGRES _ DAS _ BEGOT
```

Pardon My French

```
B A N A N A S · A S P E C T ·
A M O R I S T · T A L L I E R
F I D E L I O · L O U I S X V
F E E · · S O D · · M O T T S
I N B E D · L E C O M T E · ·
N S T A R S · S A N E · R A T
· · S T U · G N A T · N C O
C O P Y · P A R I S · A S T O
O N O · P E R I · E T C · ·
N E O · E R I E · T A R I F F
· L E S C A U T · G E N R E
A S S E T · X O X · · H A N
G U I L L O T · W E S T E N D
R E D E E M S · I N P E A C E
· R E D S E A · T O A S T E R
```

Operatic Quintet

```
P Y R E · C H A R T · V I E D
L A I C · A I R E R · A C T I
E N C H A N T E D I S L A N D
A G E O L D · N O B L E M A N
· · · I L S A · · A T E S T
J A N A C E K · S P Y · · ·
O P I N E · I O U S · L A M P
S E N T · V E R D I · U L E E
E X E S · A R E A · A L E R S
· · C T S · N A B U C C O
B L A M E · · M I L A · · ·
E U R I D I C E · I C E P O P
F I L L E D U R E G I M E N T
I S E E · O R G A N · A R I A
T A N S · L E E R S · G E T S
```

Figaro's Day of Madness

World Premieres at the Met

Over the Top

Firsts

The Rake Punished

Into the Woods